Mastermind Groups

THE FASTEST & SAFEST WAY TO GROW YOUR BUSINESS

By Moe Nawaz
Mastermind Coach

Other books byMoe Nawaz:
1. Manage Time & Grow Rich.
2. Business Growth Blueprint
3. Bankruptcy Guide
4. Insolvency Survival Guide For Businesses

Mastermind Groups

© 2011 Moe Nawaz

Cover and Interior Design by Roger Lynch

All rights reserved. No part of this publication may be reproduced or transmitted in any form or by any means, electronic or mechanical, including photocopy, recording, or any information storage and retrieval system, without permission in writing from the publisher. Printed in the United Kingdom by Bell & Bain Ltd, Glasgow

Publishers details
Help Organisation Ltd
Lawford House
Lawford Court
Birmingham. B7 4HJ
United Kingdom
Tel. 0845 430 7676
www.mastermindcoach.com

LEGAL NOTICE

This Book Is Not Legal Advice

Although I'm going to give you a lot of valuable information in this book, you must understand that this book is not legal or business advice. Moreover, reading this book will not establish a consultant–client relationship between us. The only way that I can give you legal or business advice is if you engage me. To engage me, you must sign a written agreement, called an engagement letter, which sets forth the terms of my representation of you and the details of our consultant–client relationship, including the cost.

Only after you have engaged me as your Consultant by signing an engagement letter, I will be able to give you advice. Until that time, however, I can only help you educate yourself by providing you with some useful information about mastermind groups and growing your business.

ISBN9780956485434

"Opportunities and success are both provided by our competitors"

- Moe Nawaz

Preface

"As long as a man stands in his own way, everything and everyone seems to be in his way".
Ralph Waldo Emerson

This book is a guide to building your business and growing it in the fastest, safest and the easiest ways possible by being part of a mastermind group or building your own group. It is intended to help business owners and those aspiring to start their own businesses to make smart decisions about how to build or grow their business with minimal or no risk.

The purpose of Mastermind Groups is to help business owners to exchange ideas and avoid the pitfalls. My purpose in writing *Mastermind Groups* book is to provide you with actionable, evidence-based advice on how to capitalize fully from mastermind groups while avoiding costly mistakes. This book will give you and other result based business owners powerful yet simple methods and ideas to stack the success deck in your favour. You will learn how a mastermind group or mastermind coach can demonstrably raise your performance for maximum impact. This book will help you confidently and profitably distinguish quality mastermind groups and coaches – from the rest.

When speaking at seminars about business growth to business and professional groups, journalists and television anchors, and graduate students in the UK and abroad, I encounter the same interest, the same reservations and misconceptions, the same knowledge void about sharing idea with like minded people in mastermind groups. In writing this book I've held nothing back. To the contrary, I have packed it with proven, step by step information about mastermind groups and coaches so that you – the business owner, manager, or the group coordinator - can make winning decisions quickly and confidently about joining the right mastermind group or hiring the right mastermind coach for your business.

You will find frequently asked questions and some you might not think to ask and insider tips. I share cases and success stories drawn from my experience as a business turnaround expert and a mastermind coach, helping business owners succeed through difficult times since 1989.

You can read this book from cover to cover for a complete guide to mastermind groups or you can turn to chapters selectively based on your interests or immediate needs.

This book does not offer legal or financial advice. To get help with your unique needs and objectives, you should consult a competent professional mastermind coach.

Moe Nawaz

United Kingdom.

Acknowledgements

Mastermind Groups is the result of the extraordinary experiences and interactions I have had over the years with running my own mastermind groups online and offline, clients, professional colleagues, and the many leaders in business and also the not for profit sector, education, the students and clients who contributed to my research, one and all.

I owe a particular debt of thanks to the leaders who generously shared their time and experiences with me and whose insights appear in this book. Their participation in the projects was invaluable.

Over the years I have been very fortunate to have learned from some of the masters of our time, people such as Jay Abraham, Brian Tracy, Dan Kennedy, Bill Glazer, Richard Bandler, Jim Rohn, Tony Robbins and of course not forgetting my coach Rich Schefren the guru to the gurus.

A number of other people who helped to make this work a reality. Special recognition and thanks go to Suzanne Mcgee who helped with all the research from my seminars and scripts from my mastermind classes. Many colleagues and professional who I gave earlier drafts of manuscripts the benefit of their expertise special thanks to Rich Schefren. My family, friends and fellow Heart Of England Toastmasters who were a steady source of encouragement and interest. It is a pleasure to acknowledge their support.

My family, who now know more about mastermind groups and mastermind coaching than any other family on the planet, endured my months of writing with their customary patience and good cheers.

About The Author

There must be a reason why people say that Moe Nawaz is the most trusted Business Turnaround Expert and Mastermind Coaches in Europe. Moe has worked in the turnaround industry since 1989 as an Insolvency Auditor helping 1,000's of business owners via a free advice line ukadvice.com. His clients include high tech companies, manufacturers, financial services, entrepreneurs and family run businesses throughout Europe. Moe is the author of several books including "Bankruptcy Guide", "Business Growth Blueprint" and "Manage Time and Grow Rich" He has been featured on TV, Radio and other Media. He continues to pursue and participate in programs that are both personally enriching as well as stimulating to his business acumen, and is committed to excellence. Being a member of the Institute Of Directors and the peer advisor to Mastermind Coaching that evaluates businesses on a monthly basis. He is on the board of a number of companies as a non executive director and previously sat on the advisory board to a number of Turnaround Organisations.

"Never wish life were easier, wish you were better…"

- Jim Rohn

Since 1989, Moe has been has been involved in insolvency and business turnaround sector and has become the UK's most trusted Insolvency Auditor. By 2002 Moe had developed a system for recoding why businesses failed and the most common causes of failure. Then in 2002 Moe started to study from some of the world's top coaches and mentors who taught success. From these masters and his own success with understanding failure from his insolvency experience, Moe began to develop his systems and blueprints for business success.

In 2006 Moe started working with some of the top blue chip clients in the UK sharing his success system and helping these companies to grow and get paid on a results basis only, which in turn made small fortunes for his clients and himself. Since 2009 Moe turned his interests to working with smaller businesses who want to double or triple their businesses over a 3 year period or less via his Mastermind Coaching Groups around the UK. The groups consist of up to 12 members per group. Moe has three types of groups which he teaches. Group one is for businesses with less than £500,000 turn over. Group two £500,000 to £1m and Group three business with turnover £1m to £5m, all looking to double or triple their businesses in three years or less.

Moe also works with a maximum of ten select executive clients on a one on one coaching and mentoring who have businesses with more than £5m turnover and are keen to double or triple their businesses within 3 years. This he does on a profit sharing performance basis by helping bring in extra profits with minimal or no extra cost to their companies.

In addition to having attended most of the commonly known training programs, Moe reads over fifty five books a year on failure and success strategy, marketing technique, psychology, biographies, to name a few.

This is not to say that Moe has been successful in every venture he has been involved in. He is just like everyone else who has made mistakes from time to time, but there's a big difference between failure and making mistakes.

In addition to his professional activities, Moe serves as advisor to non-profit organisations with no charges, working with them to improve operational and financial performance. Moe enjoys his weekend golfing activities and can be seen at corporate and charity golfing day.

Contents

Chapter 1 -	History of Mastermind Groups	10
Chapter 2 -	What is a Business Mastermind Group?	22
Chapter 3 -	Ten Myths About Mastermind Groups	30
Chapter 4 -	What is a Business Mastermind Coach?	38
Chapter 5 -	Why Over 90% of Businesses Fail in the First 5 Years	44
Chapter 6 -	Benefits of Joining a Mastermind Group	52
Chapter 7 –	The Different Types of Mastermind Groups	62
Chapter 8 -	What Type and Size of Business is a Good Candidate for Mastermind Groups	68
Chapter 9 -	How Do I Find a Mastermind Group to Join?	74
Chapter 10 -	How Do I Start a Mastermind Group?	82
Chapter 11 -	Who Should I Invite Into My Mastermind Group?	92
Chapter 12 -	Qualities of the People in Successful Mastermind Groups	100
Chapter 13 –	Key Qualities of a Mastermind Coach	110
Chapter 14 -	How to Maximize Your Return From a Mastermind Group	118

Chapter 15 -	Proactive vs. Reactive Mastermind Groups	126
Chapter 16 -	How a Mastermind Group Can Change and Grow Your Business	134
Chapter 17 -	**(Case Studies)** Turning an Average Business Into a Success Story with a Mastermind Group	150
Chapter 18 -	What to do next	182
Chapter 19 -	FAQs	186

Chapter 1 - History of Mastermind Groups

"You can get everything in life you want,
if you'll just help enough other people get what they want."
- Zig Zigler

Many people think of Napoleon Hill and his classic book *Think and Grow Rich* as the inception of the mastermind group concept. While the 1937 book certainly brought the idea out into the open and is used as a starting point for many people as they look to what a mastermind group is, the mastermind group existed long before Hill's bestselling book.

Napoleon Hill DOES deserve credit for bringing mastermind groups in to the mainstream and promoting the concept. In fact, that was Andrew Carnegie's hope when he asked Hill if he was ready to spend 20 or so years preparing to take Mr. Carnegie's success formula to the world.

Andrew Carnegie was a poor Scottish immigrant who rose to be the richest man in the world. He attributed much of his success to consistently surrounding himself with people who knew more than he did – and he consistently learned from them.

Mr. Carnegie's first business mastermind group was called the "Chicago 6". Other members included William Wrigley Jr. (the founder of Wrigley Chewing Gum), John R. Thompson (owner of a chain of lunchrooms), Albert Lasker (owner of the Lord & Thomas ad agency, the largest ad agency in the world at the time), Mr. McCullough (owner of the Parmalee Express Company), and William Hertz and Mr. William C. Ritchi (the owners of the Yellow Cab Company). The Chicago 6 was formed in the 1920s. Most members had no advanced education. They were self-made men, yet they were smart enough to know they could learn much from others. Within the group, they were able to share their business ideas and get feedback from the others in the group – both good and bad.

Andrew Carnegie was Napoleon Hill's mentor. When Hill was just a boy, Carnegie shared his success formula with him. After agreeing to Mr. Carnegie's request to share his formula with the world, Hill interviewed over 500 businessmen and literally dedicated his life to sharing their stories and messages to people of all walks of life. The aspect that Hill often is most associated with is the mastermind section in Chapter 9. It is titled, *The Power of the Master Mind*.

Again, while this is the start of what may be known as the beginning of the promotion of the mastermind group in a formal sense, the mastermind group concept had been around long before Mr. Carnegie and Mr. Hill popularized it in the books "Think and Grow Rich" or "The Law of Success".

Some say that the mastermind group goes back as far as Alexander the Great and his council. Others note that Socrates and his Academy were a mastermind group. Some even point out that Jesus and his disciples were a mastermind group. The founding fathers of the United States were certainly a mastermind group as they discussed the issues that confronted a burgeoning colony and how to transition from a colony to a country.

Here are some other mastermind groups throughout history that were formed to help the members of a group learn from each other...to help the members come together, as Napoleon Hill said, *"No two minds ever come together without thereby creating a third, invisible, intangible force, which may be likened to a third mind."*

The Junto

Benjamin Franklin started a group known as "The Junto" in 1727. Franklin specifically wanted it to be comprised of working men, not elite society members. Together, the members of the group would discuss issues ranging from philosophical matters to what was going on in business and politics. Franklin deeply valued this mastermind group and described the Junto in his autobiography:

"I should have mentioned before, that, in the autumn of the preceding year, I had formed most of my ingenious acquaintance into a club of mutual improvement, which we called the Junto. We met on Friday evenings. The rules that I drew up required that every member, in his turn, should produce one or more queries on any point of Morals, Politics, or Natural Philosophy, to be discussed by the company; and once in three months produce and read an essay of his own writing, on any subject he pleased. Our debates were to be under the direction of a president and to be conducted in the sincere spirit of inquiry after truth, without fondness for dispute, or desire of victory..."

It is interesting to note that just as Franklin's Junto was under the direction of a president, the mastermind groups of today are under the direction of a group leader, facilitator or moderator.

It was vitally important to Franklin that the mastermind group not turn into a contentious debate in any way. Having a president was one way of ensuring that. Another way was dictating that anyone who violated that rule be charged with a small fine.

Franklin's Junto lasted for over 30 years. It was so popular that members formed their own spin-off groups under Franklin's approval. The ideas that were spurred and fostered under these mastermind groups are often attributed to Franklin alone; however, they were the result of the power of the group. They included the volunteer fire department, the subscription library, police departments, paved streets and the public hospital.

The Metaphysical Club

The Metaphysical Club was an informal group of mental giants that met for about nine months starting in 1872. The group included Oliver Wendell Holmes Jr. (a legendary legal mind), William James (the father of modern psychology), and Charles Sanders Pierce (scientist and founder or semiotics). The Metaphysical mastermind group was set up for the purpose of exploring ideas.

The Invention Factory

Thomas Edison is known for inventing the light bulb, but he is also known for being a master inventor. He holds a total of 1,093 patents with his name on them. Edison was a strong believer in the mastermind group. He set up a group in 1887 known as the Invention Factory. He brought together some of the best minds he could find with people having different areas of expertise. They worked together in teams on various projects. Over half the patents with Thomas Edison's name on them are in fact products of the Invention Factory and the 44 years of the mastermind groups that brought forth visionary ideas and projects.

The Vagabonds

The Vagabonds was an unlikely name for an extraordinary group of men that formed a mastermind group around 1915. The group included Henry Ford (the automobile maker), Harvey Firestone (the tire mogul), Thomas Edison (the inventor), Thomas Burroughs (the naturalist) and a rotation of other members including Presidents Calvin Coolidge and Warren G. Harding and agriculturist Luther Burbank.

Although each of them were extraordinary men in their own right, they deeply valued the input of the others and looked forward to spending time with one another. Instead of meeting together in the exotic locations they all could surely have afforded, they instead chose to road-trip each summer from state to state in rustic campsites! Hence their name: The Vagabonds.

They found that the outdoors and the gypsy-style travelling was the best way for them to be inspired. They would have impromptu tree chopping and climbing contests during the day and at night would sit around the campfire. They would talk about politics, business, science – anything and everything that was going on in their lives. They could discuss their ideas openly with one another without the pressures of the outside world. It was perfect for them. The trips continued until 1924. The press eventually found out and the Vagabonds were swarmed by reporters and photographers.

President Harding had also passed away, and they decided not to continue with the road trips. Instead they continued to meet for several years at Ford's estate.

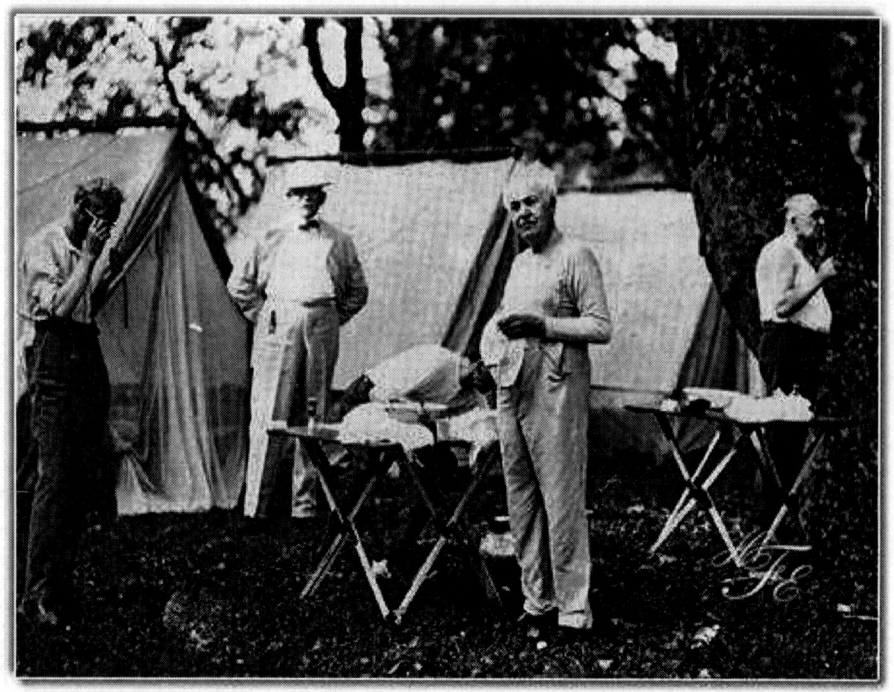

Camping in 1921 in the Great Smokies. Left to right: Ford, Bishop William F. Anderson, Firestone (stooping), Edison and Harding.

The Inkling

The Inkling was a mastermind group made of great poets and writers in Oxford, England that was formed around 1933. It included such literary greats as CS Lewis, JRR Tolkien, Charles Williams, and Owen Barfield.

In Lewis' rooms at Magdalen College or at a local pub called The Eagle and Child, the members of the Inkling would read aloud from their most recent writings. Other members would then offer up their critiques and comments on the writings. Remember, these were not just any literary works! At the time, Lewis was working on *The Screwtape Letters* and Tolkien was working on *The Hobbit*. These were other literary greats who were giving their two cents. Lewis once said that the final works of all the members owed *"a good deal to the hard hitting criticism of the circle. The problems of narrative as such -- seldom heard of in modern critical writings -- were constantly before our minds."* Interesting to think what the works may have been without the mastermind group.

The Inkling did not stick with talking just about literature. They would also discuss philosophy, faith and culture. The meetings in Lewis' rooms at the college lasted until 1949 – which coincided with Tolkien finishing *The Lord of the Rings*. The informal meetings at the pub went on until Lewis' death in 1963.

The Influence of the Internet

The influence of the Internet has changed mastermind groups dramatically. No longer do members have to meet in person or be local. Mastermind groups can consist of members all over the world who meet over the phone or via the Internet. They can still offer the support and ideas of a traditional mastermind group, but do it in a different way.

With the growing number of internet entrepreneurs, mastermind groups have become increasing valuable. When a business owner is an online or internet entrepreneur, it is easy to feel "alone". Sometimes they literally are all alone. The mastermind group is an extremely valuable way to bring together other people in the same situation to brainstorm and come up with ideas to move their business forward; especially when they are led by mastermind group leaders who have blazed a path before them. Successful mastermind leaders include Rich Schefren, Jay Abraham, Dan Kennedy, Frank Kern and Eben Pagan… But to name a few.

This book will delve in to mastermind groups in to depth, but here are a few of the thoughts of the leaders in the internet marketing space on mastermind group.

Rich Schefren – *The Guru to the Guru's* - Here are the basics of what Rich believes a mastermind group should consist of:

Size of group: Best to have about six to eight people in the group to bring in plenty of ideas to the mastermind group, but not too many to make the process overwhelming.

Process: Divide the meeting into four segments of 15 minutes each.

1. The person seeking advice describes the process in as much detail as they can.

2. The other mastermind group members ask their questions to find out more detail and to increase their understanding of the problem.

3. Now that they are fully informed and understand, the mastermind group offers up suggestions and ideas to solve the problem.

4. In the final segment, the person with the problem picks out the best ideas and makes a commitment to take certain action between this meeting and the next meeting.

Rich has run MANY mastermind groups. These are his suggestions for running a group, but he runs highly successful and sought after in-person and telephone mastermind groups for those in the internet marketing space.

Frank Kern/Jeff Walker – Both Frank and Jeff (and sometimes Rich, too!) do a different spin on the mastermind group. They will take a small group of people (like-minded as always) that have to apply to be in the mastermind group. These people must already be successfully running a business.

Their mastermind groups are often run in person over the course of 2-3 days every 3 months or so. In between the in person meetings, they will have phone meetings as well as email meetings.

They have established a sense of eliteness when it comes to their mastermind group. It's not easy to get it. You really have to want it. But you sure get a WHOLE LOT out of it! You are surrounded by the best of the best. Why? Because everyone else is EXTREMELY serious and committed as well. People are flying in from all over the U.S., and sometimes from all over the world, to be a part of their mastermind group.

So while Napoleon Hill may be considered the "grandfather" of the mastermind group – there have been great men both before and after him who have used the mastermind group to bring together great minds to accomplish great ideas.

Hill knew this. He knew that the mastermind was not only the key to Andrew Carnegie's success; he believed it to be the success of ALL great men…and that it COULD be the key to success for ANYONE, if they would but use it.

History of our Characters

As we go through this book, we are going to be following two characters as they learn about and apply mastermind group theory and practices to their business. I hope that you will be able to see how the mastermind group helps them, and how it can help your business as well.

TOBY – *Toby is 35 years old. He has an established business (12 years old) wherein he builds custom saltwater fish aquariums for businesses and homes and services them if needed. Toby has an excellent reputation in the community he lives in. He grows his own coral and has a vast knowledge of sea life. His aquariums are unique. His business has expanded to the point that he cannot handle the 90 mile area he services by himself. He uses two of his brother-in-laws, but they are not always reliable. He has recently decided to also open a brick and mortar aquarium shop with his wife. He is nervous about the amount of money they are putting into the shop. He also doesn't want the time his is putting into the shop to affect the relationships he has with his current client base.*

ANDREA – *Andrea is a 44 year old single mother of 5. She has been a special education teacher for 15 years. She's ready to move on to something else and wants to be able to spend more time with her kids. She has saved up enough money to quit her teaching job for a year and give her an online business a go. She has done extensive research and training in internet marketing and wants to launch a website with information products for parents of autistic children. While she has the basic knowledge, she does not have the experience and is nervous about actually pushing the button to "go". What if she fails?!?*

What is YOUR history??
Your Notes

"The proper functionof a business is to thrive & prosper, not just survive. I have seen too many failures just trying to survive"

— Moe Nawaz

Chapter 2 - What is a Business Mastermind Group?

"Coming together is a beginning: Keeping together is progress: Working together is success.

- Henry Ford

We've spent a lot of time talking about the history of the mastermind group – but let's back up a bit a talk about what exactly IS a mastermind group. As mentioned earlier, the mastermind concept is often contributed to Napoleon Hill. In his book *Think and Grow Rich*, Hill defines a mastermind as a *"coordination of knowledge and effort, in a spirit of harmony, between two or more people, for the attainment of a definite purpose."*

A little more simply put…two minds are better than one. Better yet, when you bring several minds together, and they are working on a common goal, a synergy happens within the group that could not happen with one person by himself. In other words, "The whole is greater than the sum of the parts." That is the power of the mastermind.

A good mastermind group will allow the participants to come together and discuss and idea or ideas about their business. This may include a specific business idea such as marketing for an upcoming holiday, or it can be something more broad, such as how to balance work and life as a business person.

The members of the group offer suggestions, insight and support to each other that they would not normally receive. This is not a "support group" and it's not a "networking group". It goes far beyond that. It is about having a solid group of like-minded people working on a common goal and sharing experiences to help one another achieve those goals. There is a GOAL at the end. Not just a "talk session".

So let's move this forward to a typical business mastermind group of today. Here are some of the components that make up a mastermind group:

GOAL

In a nutshell, a business mastermind group is a group of like-minded business individuals with a common goal who meet together on a regular basis to brainstorm, support and assist one another. For business members, mastermind groups can provide support, motivation, inspiration, problem-solving, encouragement and ideas.

The goal of the mastermind group as a whole should be as defined as possible. "To have a successful business" is not a strongly defined goal. However, "Increasing the profitability of each member of the group by a minimum of 20% in 2012" is a more precise goal, then helping each member to breaking it down to smaller but manageable chunks, so that the goals can be achieved not just visualized.

The mastermind group has the ability to see things from a grander perspective. Even better, as different minds start talking and expounding on ideas, others will chime in and new ideas will form. You may find yourself coming up with an idea that never occurred to you before as you are inspired from the synergy in the group. Or you may be that inspiration to another member in the group.

NUMBER OF ATTENDEES

In a typical business mastermind group, there are a set number of attendees that may join the group. The number is usually kept small enough to ensure that everyone can participate. "Small" means that a typical group will usually consist of somewhere between 4 and 12 people. You need to have enough people so that there is interaction and ideas are flowing. However, if there are TOO many people in the group, not everyone gets a chance to get voice their opinions or bring up their challenges.

Each group really differs in finding their "sweet spot" with regard to the number of participants that fit that particular group. It is easier to start on a smaller scale and see how it works and then add participants if the group is functioning well. This is much easier than having too many participants in the beginning and finding that people are frustrated because they feel they don't have a chance to participate.

Also, keep in mind that vacations and other issues do come up. If you have a group that is too small, you may find yourself with only two or three attendees for some of your sessions. While you can still have a mastermind session, it's not as productive as having more members there to fully bounce ideas and suggestions around.

FACILITATOR

There is often a facilitator or a moderator of the group. We'll be talking more about the benefits of having a facilitator or a moderator for the group in a later chapter.

AGENDA

The agenda may be up to the group. It usually consists of a small period of introduction, and then time to go through each person's "issue". Or you may choose to have a hot seat topic. We will discuss these options more in a later chapter.

FULL PARTICIPATION

One thing is vitally important, and that is EVERYONE in the group must participate. Your peers will be giving you feedback, and they will expect your feedback in return. It is only through full participation that the group will truly be able to fully attain new heights. As an individual business person, it is easy to get caught up in seeing things one way. You are close to your project, you visualized it from its inception, and you simply can't see it from another direction. By being able to see it from a fresh set of eyes, someone who is totally from another sector to yours – you will learn how to adopt new ways of exploding your business and not just what everyone in your industry is doing.

ACCOUNTABILITY

The business mastermind group is also about accountability. It is easy as a business person (especially as a solo entrepreneur) to put off setting goals, or to justify not hitting goals. Soon you can find yourself losing any form of accountability. In a business mastermind group, you will be setting up, focusing on and tracking your accountability systems. You'll find yourself more inspired than ever to do so when you have a support system and the group behind you. Feeling like you're "not in it alone" can be a tremendous weight off your shoulders. Knowing that you have someone to report in to and bounce ideas off can also be a huge motivation!

TOBY – Toby can see that the mastermind group concept might be of worth for him. He has built his business on his own – from trial and error. His wife has been his webmaster and accountant and they've done a pretty darn good job. But he's never really had anyone else to bounce ideas off of. He is interested in the part of having someone see things from a different perspective. He'd love to have someone's perspective of how he is going to run his "regular" business while growing his brick and mortar business. Does everyone else think he's just nuts? Should he continue using his brothers-in-law?

The other thing Toby is really thinking might work for him is the accountability perspective. Toby has always been a procrastinator. Yes, it's always driven his wife nuts. His wife giving him a deadline really hasn't worked for him. Maybe having accountability to a mastermind group will make a difference. Maybe it would even bring more peace to his home as well as growth to his business. That would be a bonus!!

ANDREA - The thought of having support, motivation, inspiration and ideas sounds JUST right for Andrea. While she is very excited about the prospect of starting this new business venture and she KNOWS she is fully capable, self doubt likes to creep into her head constantly. She knows that having a support system will be vital to her. She does better when she has people cheering her on, and she knows she'll be alone for much of this journey.

Accountability is another aspect that appeals to Andrea. After all, she is a single mother of 5. Things can easily get in the way of her progress. At least she can LET things get in the way if she's not careful. But if she knows that she will be checking in with a mastermind group, it will keep her on-task and motivated. She doesn't like being the person in the group who hasn't made progress.

What appeals to YOU about the mastermind group?
Your Notes:

"I am an old man and have a great many troubles, but most of them never happened"

– Mark Twain

Chapter 3 - Ten Myths About Mastermind Groups

"New doubt that a small group of thoughtful, committed citizen can change the world. Indeed it is the only thing that ever has."

- Margaret Mead

It's interesting to hear of people who may have been in a mastermind group in the past or have heard of mastermind groups who have a negative opinion of them. In most cases I find that any negative opinions are due to someone having been in a mastermind group that wasn't TRULY run as a "mastermind group". Anyone can call a get-together a mastermind group, but that doesn't mean they are a true mastermind group in the spirit of what a mastermind group is meant to be.

Over the years, I've heard plenty of "myths" about what mastermind groups are.

1. **You Don't Have to Participate in the Mastermind Group** – If you've been in a group where there has been a person that regularly does not participate, you know that it is very frustrating. It's hard to feel comfortable sharing when you don't feel like everyone else is doing the same. The mastermind group doesn't seem to "gel" when there isn't full participation by all members. If there is a member that isn't participating, it can ruin the whole group, and quite honestly, they should be asked to leave. You DO have an obligation to participate in the mastermind group.

2. **A Mastermind Group Doesn't Have Clear Goals** – If a mastermind group is meeting together without a clear set of goals, it is not a mastermind group. There is not any ONE goal, but the group does have to decide what the goals are as a whole. It could be to increase the profitability of the business of the group members. That may differ for each member in the group, but there is still a common goal. The goal should be identified and then re-addressed on a regular basis to ensure the group is moving towards that goal. If the group feels like it needs to readdress or add another goal that is okay, as long as there is consensus within the group.

3. **There Are Not Rules in a Mastermind Group** – If you've been in a group like this, I'm sure it has been very frustrating. There must be rules, they must be written down, and the members must abide by them. If members are allowed to show up whenever they want, for instance, it's very hard to create a feeling of trust among the members in the group. Some groups will have a "three strikes and you're out" policy. There are sample guidelines for a mastermind group later in the book. Make sure your mastermind group has a set of rules or guidelines. Again, the rules are agreed upon by the members in the group.

4. **Mastermind Groups are Expensive** – The cost of a mastermind group varies. Some are free; some cost a fair amount of money. You can look around to find a group that fits your needs depending on the business people involved and your goals. If you are looking for a group that is led by a professional coach, there will be a cost, but there are also added benefits. We will discuss that in a later chapter. Realize however that the costs vary greatly. If you don't find a group that fits your needs, you can start your own.

5. **One Person Ends Up Talking the Whole Time** – This is NOT what a mastermind group should be. If you've been in one like this, it was not run correctly. In a well-run mastermind group, EVERYONE has the opportunity to address their issue and everyone has an opportunity to give their input on the issue being discussed. There should never be a "floor hog". The

mastermind coach should be moderating the session to watch this closely. If you join a mastermind group where you feel someone is running with too much time, approach the coach. If it doesn't change, switch to a different mastermind group.

6. **A Mastermind Group is Really Just a Networking Opportunity** – This couldn't be further from the truth. Yes, the members of the group will probably end up networking with each other and bringing business to each other. But that is NOT the purpose of the group. If that is the reason anyone joins the group, they are not going to reach their goal. Not only that, they have seriously treated the others in the group with great disrespect and once the others realize it, they have certainly done JUST THE OPPOSITE for their business. The mastermind group is not about growing your business, but about coming up with ideas generated by other great minds. Not by "using" each other.

7. **Mastermind Groups Don't Have Agendas** – Well, let me say this…successful mastermind groups DO have agendas. I will say that one of the top reasons I see people dropping out of mastermind groups is there not being an agenda. When the group does not have structure and falters each meeting with no direction, people don't tend to come back. Ask what the agenda is before you join a mastermind group.

8. **A Mastermind Group is a Presentation** – It most certainly is not. You should not be talked AT by a presenter during a mastermind group. You should be part of a group discussion. That being said, SOME mastermind groups will have a presentation in the beginning. This may be to have some education and get the dialogue going on a specific business topic. It's a great way to dig deep into a subject after learning more about it. But the entire session will never be JUST a presentation where you are talked to, or it's not a mastermind group!

9. **Group Size Doesn't Matter** – It certainly DOES matter. The dynamics of the group are better is it stays with 12 or fewer people in the group. Larger is not better in this case. Everyone needs the time to be able to speak and be heard. Some people

will mastermind with as few as two people; however, four is a good minimum number for a group to have good interaction.

10. **Mastermind Groups Aren't Effective** – Mastermind groups are one of the MOST effective things you can do for your business. You'll see in stories in a later chapter how effective they have been for others. I have seen them make a difference in business after business, large and small.

TOBY: *The "myth" that Toby had heard and made him most wary of mastermind groups is that the group is a presentation. He felt he really didn't have time to just be "talked at" for two hours. He was really looking for interaction, ideas and support in his business. If he could find that in a mastermind group, he'd be open to it.*

ANDREA: *The "myth" that Andrea most identified with was that mastermind groups don't have an agenda. As a previous teacher, meetings without agendas drive her CRAZY. She likes organization. She doesn't have time to waste on people sitting around wondering what to do next. She wants a clear plan of action. If she is involved in a mastermind group that runs efficiently, she will be happy to stay with it.*

What myth do you most identify with?

What has kept you from joining a mastermind group in the past?

Your Notes:

"A winner knows how much he still has to learn, even when he is considered an expert by others. A loser wants to be considered an expert by others before he has learned enough to know how little he knows"

— Sydney Harris

Chapter 4 - What is a Business Mastermind Coach?

"Seek the counsel of [those] who will tell you the truth about yourself, even if it hurts you to hear it.

Mere commendation will not bring the improvement you need.

– Napoleon Hill

Any good business mastermind group will have a business mastermind coach. I often get the question "What is a business mastermind coach and why does our mastermind group need one?"

Business Coach

I first want to address the idea of a business coach in general. You may think, "I'm in business. I'm a business person. I know what it means to run a business. I certainly don't need a coach." Think of this for a moment. There are professional golfers that certainly know their game. They make a LOT of money hitting a ball into a hole. Yet they still have a coach that helps them with their swing...making it even better.

Why? A golf coach can see things they can't see. They have a different perspective. The same thing is true with a business coach. They help you to see things from a different perspective – they encourage you to try things from a different point of view.

Another thing that a coach does for an athlete is helps to keep them accountable. No smart athlete would dare keep their coach waiting. They show up when they are supposed to and when they don't perform up to snuff, they have their coach to report to.

A business coach can provide the same accountability for a business owner. Together, the coach and business owner can set goals. There is an accountability system put in to place and the business owner has to report it. If they don't do what they say they were going to do, they better have a good reason why. Being a solo entrepreneur often means being able to justify putting things off. Even in large corporate environments you will find coaches and mentors (believe me it is so lonely at the top, I have seen it so many times) It gets a little too easy sometimes! Having a coach whom you are accountable to can really help.

Mastermind Business Coach

Now a mastermind business coach differs a bit from a regular business coach. They are not going to be coaching you through aspects of your business. They are going to have more of a silent kind of role...more of a moderator or facilitator role in the mastermind group.

However, they do still provide that excellent bird's eye view and different perspective. They can ask an open-ended question that gets the group off and talking on a subject. They can help clarify a question or issue that someone seems to have trouble putting into words. They can also help to ensure that everyone is having an opportunity to be heard.

A mastermind business coach is vital in having a mastermind group run smoothly. Having a mastermind business coach is often the difference between having a group that is efficient and productive and one that is frustrating and ends up dissolving after a few sessions.

TOBY: *To be perfectly honest, Toby didn't even realize there were such things as businesses coaches or mastermind coaches. He doesn't really understand why either one would be important since he's made it 12 years without one.*

However, thinking about it just a little deeper, he has been a soccer coach for 13 years. And he couldn't imagine any individual being able to make it without a coach. Not just from a team perspective, but from an individual perspective as well. So maybe there is something to it after all...he'll stay open-minded.

ANDREA: *As Andrea has done quite a bit of research on her internet business, she's read quite a bit about business coaches and the difference they can make for a person's business. She loves the fact that they can help with a different perspective – that is something that she feels she will really need.*

Andrea is a very organized person. She definitely sees the value in a mastermind coach. She does would not want to be in a group where there was not one. She understands the value of having a person to guide the group. She wants a mastermind group that is productive and efficient and she knows it will take a strong mastermind coach as well as quality members for that to happen.

Are you familiar with the concept of business and mastermind coaches?

How do you feel about the importance of a mastermind coach for your mastermind group?

Your Notes:

"Ninety percent of all those who fail are not actually defeated. They simply quit"

– Paul j. Meyer

Chapter 5 - Why Over 90% of Businesses Fail in the First 5 Years

"We all have to decide how we are going to fail... by not going far enough or by going too far."

– Summer Redstone

Before we go any further in exploring mastermind groups, I'd like to take some time to take a look at a VERY important statistic. I'm sure you've heard variations of this, but the bottom line is that over 90% of businesses fail in the first five years.

But here is something even more startling. A study by Duns and Bradstreet the world's largest commercial credit reference agency found that "90% of small businesses that fail do so because of a lack of skills and knowledge on the part of the owner." Think about this for a minute. We like to blame the economy or location or the competition for the failure of a business…especially if it's our own! But 90% fail to do so because of a lack of skills and knowledge of the part of the owner?!? That's fixable!

Skills and knowledge can be GAINED. But here's another interesting statistic from Harvard University – only 10% of us are "natural learners". That means people that naturally seek out information on a consistent basis. The other 90%? Well, they just don't. They may be forced to from time to time, but it doesn't come natural to them.

So let's put these two statistics together and sort out what they really mean for an average business owner. The AVERAGE business owner lacks the skills and knowledge to run a business properly. FURTHERMORE, the same average business owner is not wired to naturally seek out the information that is out there and available to gain the skills and knowledge to run their business properly. *No wonder most businesses fail!!!*

Here are some of the common areas that business owners lack skills and knowledge in:

1. **Business Planning** – I've seen it plenty of times. A business owner goes in to a business without a definitive plan. Whether it's 2-page plan or a 50-page plan – there MUST be a plan. You need to have a vision, goals and milestones. It will help you to keep your focus and to raise the red flag if you are off track before it gets too late. The business plan should be reviewed and modified at least on a yearly basis.

2. **Marketing** – Just because you have a "really great idea about getting customers" doesn't mean you know about marketing. You need to keep up on the marketing scene, especially in today's exploding internet marketing, social media and mobile marketing arenas. Just because something seems "new fangled" or "hard to understand" doesn't mean it's not for you. You can get left behind very quickly.

3. **Record keeping/finances** – This is not the "fun" part of the business (unless you always had a secret dream to be an accountant). But it is absolutely necessary to have your finger on the financial pulse of your business at all times. This means P&L's, expense reports, taxes…and if you don't know what I'm talking about, get help NOW.

4. **Money management** – You may think this is the same thing as #3, but it's different. You need to know how to manage the money of your business and to make wise decisions with regard to where your money goes. What is the ROI associated with a particular money decision? Are you reinvesting profit back into your business or just using it to live off of? You need to make sure you are setting realistic budgets for your business and your personal life.

5. **Time management** – The majority of entrepreneurs I work with struggle with time management in one way or another. Some struggle with procrastination or time wasting. Others struggle with putting too MUCH time in to their business and not enjoying their home and personal life. Both can cause serious problems in the long term viability and health of a business and its owner. See my other products on time management **"Manage Time And Grow Rich"**.

6. **Customer service** – Let's face it – not everyone is a people person! The bottom line is that it will always be easier to keep a current customer than to acquire a new one…as long as you develop and maintain good customer service. Bad customer service will sink your business quickly.

7. **Sales techniques** – It doesn't do you any good to have a product or service if you don't know how to get people to buy it! You don't have to be a "snake oil salesman", but some people are so afraid of being labelled a "salesman" that they don't SELL at all! Sales techniques are all about finding the needs of your customers and meeting them with your product or service. Every business owners need to learn to sell, be it a product or a service, we all need to sell in some form or other.

8. **Technical knowhow** – Most businesses need a website, social marketing, landing pages, and other techie "stuff". You don't have to do it all, but you better make sure you at least know what it is and have someone who can do it for you.

9. **Inventory management** – If you are a business that has an inventory, you'd better be competent at managing it. Having items sitting on your shelf for 2 years will NOT be helpful to your bottom line.

10. **Staff management and training** – If you are a larger company that has even ONE other employee, you'd better have a training system in place. You can never assume that one person will be the only person working for you. You also want to make sure you have a clearly defined management style. Are you laid back? Expect people to be punctual? You can't be one way one day and something else another. Consistency is key.

Now that we've identified the areas that many business owners lack skills and knowledge in, let's go back to the concept of the mastermind group. A particular business owner may not have ALL of the skills and knowledge needed to run their business, but guess what? The chances are pretty good that if they join a mastermind group, there is someone else in the group that has a skill set or knowledge in an area where they are lacking.

The great part of it is you don't have to go to a formal class to learn these things (although you can...). You can learn from other business owner who have literally "been there" and "done that". Often times this can be from several other business owners within the group. You can bounce ideas around, learn from what has worked for others, and maybe even develop something new that you can try for yourself, based on the experience of others.

With a solid mastermind group, there is no reason for YOU to be one of the 90% of businesses that fail due to a lack of skills or knowledge on the part of the business owner. You may lack them, but you can acquire or learn them before it's too late!

TOBY: Toby is actually very lucky when it comes to his business! He DOES lack a great many of the skills and knowledge listed above. He's survived the 12 years in his business so far by doing well in the areas that he thrives in. He is excellent in his knowledge of his product and service and his customer service skills are fantastic. His wife has done an excellent job at the financial record keeping, so there has never been a problem knowing where they are in their business.

Here are some of the skills and knowledge where Toby is not so great:

- **Business planning** – Toby and his wife have never done a business plan. It's always been a "fly by the seat of their pants" business. No real goals. When they decided to open the aquarium store, there was not a plan in place for how to handle the building and servicing of on-site aquariums. Nor are there any financial goals or milestones set.
- **Time management** – Definitely a problem for Toby. He coaches soccer and is president of a local soccer league. He is constantly spending either too much or too little time on his business. He always feels like he's running late and never has time to relax and enjoy life.
- **Inventory management** – The retail store will be new territory for Toby. He's a little nervous about making sure he has enough…but not too much inventory for his customers.
- **Staff management and training** – Not only does Toby struggle with his brothers-in-law, but now he will have to hire, train and manage staff at the aquarium shop as well.

ANDREA: Andrea knows that she has a lot to learn about running a business after being an educator. She is a "natural learner" and has taken the time to seek and learn many aspects about being an entrepreneur. She has a solid business plan and she knows that time management is a particular strength of hers – it's had to be with juggling work and 5 kids and all their activities! However, she realizes that nothing takes the place of actual experience, and she knows that while she may have some book knowledge of a variety of subjects, she still lacks some skill sets. Here are the areas that Andrea feels she lacks in:

- **Sales techniques** – Andrea has a phobia of the word "salesperson". She doesn't want to be associated with being a salesperson, yet she knows she *needs to make sales in order to run a profitable business. Andrea needs to learn the fine line of selling (negative) and meeting the needs of a potential customer (positive) and that not all sales is bad.*

- **Money management** – *Money management has never been a strength of Andrea's. When you add in words like "return on investment", things get a little fuzzy. She is also worried about business and personal blending in to each other and how she will be able to manage that properly.*

- **Marketing** – *While Andrea feels that she has a solid product and a good initial marketing plan, one of her biggest fears is that she doesn't have enough marketing ideas once the original idea runs its course. She feels like a few more multi-dimensional marketing ideas would be good to have in her "back pocket".*

As we continue through the chapters, we'll be keeping track of how Toby and Andrea are doing with their business weaknesses as they explore the mastermind groups and how they may be able to help them as they have identified their weaknesses.

Think about the areas that you lack skills or knowledge in your business.

What areas do you need to improve your skills or knowledge in your business?

Your Notes:

> *"Don't let your learning lead to knowledge; let your learning lead to action"*
>
> — Jim Rohn

Chapter 6 - Benefits of Joining a Mastermind Group

"None of us is as smart as all of us."

– **Ken Blanchard**

The benefits of joining a mastermind group vary from one person to another. What one person REALLY needs and benefits from may be entirely different from another member in the same group. Just look at the needs in the previous chapter to get an idea of what skills and knowledge are necessary! There are other benefits of joining a group as well. Here are some of the most common benefits I have found for business clients and members that join a mastermind group:

- **Accountability** – As mentioned earlier, one of the biggest negatives of being an entrepreneur can be the lack of accountability. A favourite sign of mine is *"If at first you don't succeed, deny you were ever trying."* Not because I believe in it, but because I've seen so many entrepreneurs who live it! With a good mastermind group, they CAN'T live it! The group holds you accountable to what you say you are going to do. When you know you're going to be meeting with your mastermind group in a few days, you make SURE you have something positive to report on your progress.

Imagine as a business owner making a goal in front of your peers in your mastermind group to come up with your 3rd quarter marketing plan by the time you meet for your next mastermind session. As the time comes closer and you've not done anything (procrastination and time management may be an issue for you) the thought of being in front of your peers and telling them you didn't do ANYTHING sinks in. You know and respect the others in this group. It's not going to feel good to be "that one" who never does what they say they are going to do. So you have two options: 1) Make progress on your plan or 2) Don't go to your mastermind group session.

Not going doesn't make any sense! You're losing out on other valuable information for your business. So what makes the most sense? Work on your marketing plan. Not JUST because you'll look better in front of your group…but more importantly because it's IMPORANT for your business! The accountability just helps to push you to do those important things!

- **Personal Growth** – As you participate on a regular basis and learn that you have as much to GIVE as you have to gain (this specially goes for me too, I am learning all the time from all my mastermind groups and my coaching and mentor clients), you will acquire additional self-worth. It doesn't matter how much confidence you had before, meeting in a group of like-minded people that have a high amount of energy will bring you a tremendous amount of personal as well as professional growth.

I've seen many people come in to a mastermind group thinking they will be learning quite a lot, but they don't have the confidence that they will be able to give much to the group. Honestly, it can be what holds some people back from joining a mastermind group – that feeling of "not being good enough". You'll be amazed at how a simple thought or idea of yours can morph into a fantastic idea with the help and power of a mastermind group. As you see ONE idea or thought that has that power, it will help you to realize that there are even MORE ideas inside you that have that power and ability.

- **Resources** – While this is not about networking for your business to "get, get, get," you will naturally find yourself on the receiving end of a tremendous amount of resources. Remember the quote in the first chapter…***"You can get everything in life you want, if you'll just help enough other people get what they want."*** It happens.

> *"The divine guidance
> often comes when
> the horizon is
> the blackest"*
>
> - Mahatma Gandhi

The great thing is, it tends to happen when you least expect it! You may be talking about an idea or concept…and you lack a key piece or resource to bring it all together. Someone in the group may say, "You know, I know just the person or just the place for that." As you expand your network, so expands your resources.

- **Differing Perspectives** – When you associate yourself with the same people day after day and year after year, you tend to take on the same perspectives. It's simply human nature. It is incredibly refreshing to belong to a mastermind group with people of differing views and perspectives. They will help you to see things in your business from a completely unique vantage point. You may find yourself trying things you would have never even imagined. It's cool!

At the same time, you can offer a completely different perspective to someone else. Sometimes your idea or thought doesn't have to be earth shattering…it's just from a different perspective. It's great to hear in a mastermind group, "You know, I never thought about it that way." I hear this again and again!

- **Mutual Support** – The mastermind group is a safe place of mutual support at all time. You will not find someone putting down your ideas. They may ask you questions or encourage you to see things from a different perspective, but there is always respect. That is something that is often lacking in today's business environment.

After tossing around an idea and looking at it from all angles, if you decide to "go for it", you'll have a group of people that will be cheering you on and rooting for your success. There is no competition in a mastermind group. Everyone wants everyone else to be successful.

- **Encouragement** – A part of most mastermind groups is a section of celebration. It is great to have the encouragement of fellow mastermind members. Hearing a "good job" or "well done" is something that may be sorely missing in your business. It can be something that you look forward to in your mastermind get together.

Be willing to share your successes, no matter how small they may seem. When you get used to celebrating each success with your mastermind group, it will help you to stay motivated with your goals and action plans. And if you're struggling, let the group know. You'll be amazed how they can find some area in your business to give you encouragement in. Staying positive is vital in your business!

- **Energy** – There may be days in your business when you frankly do not have energy. Let's face it, there may be weeks on end that the energy is lacking. A good mastermind group will bring that energy back to your business. When the ideas are flowing back and forth, a real energy is created that carries over into your business for days. It will be like a shot in the arm.

That renewed energy in your business can work wonders. Take it and make a DIFFERENCE in something that will bring in needed cash flow or revitalize your customer base.

- **Experience** – You will benefit from the years of experience within the group. There are people within the group who have "been there, done that" and you will be able to gain ideas and energy from them.

Don't take that experience for granted. Someone may have experience in business planning while someone else has experience in marketing. Another person in the group may be a whiz in internet marketing. Use all that experience to round out your business to be the best it can be.

- **Specialized Knowledge** – The same applies for specialized knowledge. As we talked about in the previous chapter, there may be parts of your business you simply need to learn MORE about. You have other business people who have that specialized knowledge that you can learn from.

If you don't use it, you're leaving that specialized knowledge on the table…leaving it to waste when you could sorely be using it!

- **Synergy** – One of the very best parts of a mastermind group! It will end up taking on a life of its own! The ideas that will come out of a mastermind group will end up being ones that weren't even on the original path, but are marvellous, productive and profitable!

The synergy is one of my favourite parts of the mastermind group. I think that's because you never know where it's going to come from or exactly what it's going to be. An idea or concept that started as one thing will morph, and morph again. It will be added to, carved and chipped away at, and turn into a life of its own. Often times something that's not even recognizable from what it started from. In fact, sometimes it has NOTHING to do with what it started from.

Yet that's okay!! Ideas that come from the synergy of the group can be incredibly dynamic. Sometimes for only one person in the group…and sometimes for many or ALL of the people in the group. Partnerships can be formed, or a new independent business can be formed. You just never know!

You are sure to find other benefits of the mastermind group that are just your own. Some you will expect; others you will not!

TOBY: *Toby can definitely see how some benefits of joining the mastermind group would apply to him. Yet he is skeptical or ambivalent to some of the others. Some he feels just don't apply to him (this is common – and many people find that the benefits they actually get from joining are different from those they expected in the beginning). Here are some of the benefits that appeal to Toby:*

- ***Accountability*** *– Procrastination is a big problem for Toby. There are a lot of projects and goals he would like to achieve with his business, but one thing or another just seems to get in the way. While he is accountable to his wife to some degree, he can still procrastinate because a lot of the "things" that get in the way are household projects, soccer (which they are both involved with), or kids events. Having other business-minded people to be accountable to would be refreshing, and hopefully motivating.*

- ***Differing Perspectives*** *– It's pretty much always been Toby and his wife who have made the business decisions. It would be interesting to see what other people have to say. His only trepidation is that other people don't know the aquarium business, but he knows he needs to open his mind and realize they may have other general business ideas that could be helpful.*

- ***Mutual Support*** *– While Toby's not a real "touchy feely" kind of guy, the fact of the matter is that there hasn't ever been anyone else to give him support in his business and to bounce ideas off of. Or to say, "Hey, that was a great job landing that account." He's kind of embarrassed to admit it, but the idea of having some mutual support sounds good!*

- ***Specialized Experience*** *– The specialized experienced that Toby could use that was discussed in the last chapter would be extremely helpful.*

- ***Energy*** *– This is another one that's hard for Toby to admit that he could use. He's a strong, athletic guy. But the days of working the business and trying to hold the family together can wear on him. Sometimes it's just not easy to have the energy in his business to be up for the customers and feel like going after new clients. Yeah, his business can use a shot of energy from time to time…it would be a good thing.*

ANDREA: *There are a lot of benefits of joining a mastermind group that Andrea thinks would be good for her personally and good for her business. She* has often struggled with self confidence. Starting a business was a big step for her, and she still wonders if it was a smart thing to do. Here are some of the benefits that Andrea identifies with:

- **Accountability** – With 5 kids and a busy life, Andrea knows that accountability will be a major help for her. Knowing that she'll be checking back in with her peers will help her to stay focused. She's a people pleaser by nature, and she will want to look good to others. That will be helpful in getting her goals and action steps done!

- **Personal Growth** – This is a big one for Andrea. She is a poster child for her insecurities getting in the way and stopping her from joining a mastermind group. Her biggest fear is that she will not have anything to contribute to the group, or what she has to say will "sound silly". Yet at the same time, she knows she is educated and intelligent. She knows that the mastermind group will be a fantastic opportunity to overcome some of her insecurities and obtain personal growth.

- **Encouragement** – Andrea knows she'll need plenty of encouragement along the way, and working from home will not be an easy way to find it! A mastermind group will be a great way to get encouragement as she makes progress with her website and even as she hits roadblocks. This is another top reason for her to consider joining a mastermind group.

- **Energy** – Working at home alone, Andrea knows she will need those energy shots for her business! She knows that starting a business is not easy. She knows there will be rough patches and she will need energy to keep going.

- **Synergy** – Andrea is actually very excited about the possibilities of the synergy of the group. She knows that is can bring exciting new ideas. She loves to help others, and she looks forward to seeing what ideas come out of the synergy of the group.

What benefits of the Mastermind group appeal to you?
Your Notes:

"Effort only fully releases its reward after a person refuses to quit"

- Napoleon Hill

Chapter 7 – The Different Types of Mastermind Groups

"There never were in the world two opinions alike, no more than two hairs or two grains; the most universal quality is diversity."

– Michel de Montainge

There are basically two **different** types of groups. The Vertical Mastermind groups which are made up of one particular type of group, industry or niche and the Horizontal Mastermind group, which is made of a variety of industries in one particular group. There can also be sub-groups in a Vertical group that can be considered more of a horizontal group. Sound confusing enough?!! I'll do my best to give you some examples and explain how they can be beneficial.

VERTICAL GROUPS

Oftentimes Vertical groups sound good at first because they truly are "like-minded people searching for a common goal." When you think of like-minded people, you tend to think of someone that you have something very much in common with. Here are some typical examples of Vertical groups:

Entrepreneurs – Entrepreneurs have a unique set of circumstances that other entrepreneurs can relate to and understand. They certainly have similar challenges and can benefit from what others have experienced or are experiencing. This is a common mastermind group.

Internet Marketers – Another group that has a very unique set of circumstances is internet marketers. They also have a very unique language and work flow that would not be common for others who are not in the IM space. They tend to enjoy a mastermind group that has others that know what they are talking about and get easily frustrated with people who don't understand the ins and outs of internet marketing.

Network Marketers – This is a group that is used to being on the "outside" in terms of respect from a lot of other businesses. Yet those who are in network marketing understand the language, the opportunities and the need for encouragement. As long as there is a clear rule of "no recruiting" among the participants, it can be a VERY productive environment for a mastermind group.

Sales People – Most sales people would love to hear more from others on how to close more deals, get more leads, convert more leads, have more renewable contracts, etc. As long as there are no competing niches of salespeople, there can be some GREAT ideas shared and the synergy that can be created from salespeople is incredible! It really is a great group to produce some fantastic campaign and lead-generating ideas.

Retirees – Retired doesn't mean done! Many retirees love getting together in a mastermind group to share...from business ideas to stock trading to investments to vacation planning. It's a great way to use the mind!

Horizontal within Vertical

This is when it gets a little more tricky!! Let's go back to Internet Marketers for instance. We can go two different ways:

1. **Strictly Vertical** – If we were going to stay strictly vertical, we would dig a little deeper and look at JUST eCommerce businesses or JUST SEO consultants for instance. The mastermind group would be very specific and would include only one type of business within internet Marketing. The internet marketers could be across the country. The benefit is that the group could really delve into the specifics of the issues that arose for them. It would be much more laser focused. The downside is that there would be less input from other perspectives.

2. **Horizontal within Vertical** – The other option with our Internet Marketers would be to have an eCommerce business owner, an informational product business owner, an SEO consultant or two, an ebook author and a membership site owner. All different type of Internet businesses. They understand the basics of Internet businesses and all have something to offer. AND…they may bring something from a past business experience that is helpful as well.

HORIZONTAL GROUPS

Horizontal groups give you the opportunity to get ideas from people from all different industries. Again, you never know what someone will bring from a past experience that you did not expect!

It's a little tougher to find the "like-minded" part of a horizontal group, so it's important that there is still some type of common goal. The like-minded can be something as simple as having a "green" philosophy or a military background....whatever is important to you. It's a start!

Or you can have a 75% vertical group and bring in some outside industry people to add a little mix to the group, as long as you have the approval of the mastermind group. Always remember, it's about meeting the needs of the group. As long as the group agrees, and it's good for the group, go for it!

TOBY: Toby decided that a horizontal mastermind group would be best for him. He wants to learn from others from a wide range of business experiences. He has no pre-conceived notions coming into the mastermind group and is just eager to learn from others.

The only thing he would like is to meet with a local group. He lives in a unique area and would like to meet with others that understand the marketing and clientele in the area.

ANDREA: Andrea would like to be in a vertical mastermind group. She thinks that a vertical mastermind group of internet marketers would be a good fit for her. She doesn't care if the group includes eCommerce, info marketers and/or affiliate marketers. However, she would like it to include some other info marketers in order to bounce some ideas off of.

Andrea would prefer to meet over the phone. She feels that she would gain valuable experience from internet marketers that aren't necessarily in her geographical area. In fact, they could even be in another part of the world!

What type of Mastermind Group do you think would be a good fit for you? Why?

Your Notes:

"By failing to prepare you are preparing to fail"

-Benjamin Franklin

Chapter 8 - What Type and Size of Business is a Good Candidate for Mastermind Groups

"Teamwork is the ability to work together toward a common vision.

The ability to direct individual accomplishments toward organizational objectives. It is the fuel that allows common people to attain uncommon results."

– Andrew Carnegie

Both small and large businesses are good candidates for a mastermind group – but in two different ways. I think it is best to look at them separately and how a mastermind can benefit each.

Small Business – A small business probably has the best flexibility in terms of a mastermind group. Any type of industry can work in a mastermind group for a small business. As we talked in the previous chapter, a small business owner can go with a vertical or a horizontal mastermind group. If they decide to go with a vertical business group, there are a variety of ways they can go…their business type, small business, gender or age-based business, location-based mastermind, and much more. Mastermind groups can also be online, so the options are unlimited!

Small businesses are often a good candidate for mastermind groups due to the fact that they are often run by an owner with little input from others in the organization. While that is positive in many ways for a small business owner, it has its drawbacks as well. There is no one to bounce ideas off of, no one to get valuable experience from, and no one to be held accountable to. All of these reasons make a small business a very good fit for joining a mastermind group.

Large Business or Organization – A large business or organization has several different options.

External Mastermind Groups – Some businesses find that sending their executives or managers to external mastermind groups helps to keep their minds fresh with new ideas. It can be difficult to come up with new ideas when you are in the same space and around the same people day in and day out. External mastermind groups have been VERY valuable. Executives and managers will often come back refreshed and with new ideas that energize the organization.

Internal Mastermind Groups – Many large organizations also find that internal mastermind groups that are run by mastermind coaches help to achieve maximum results in an internal mastermind group. An internal mastermind group can help employees bust through "old thinking" and come up with new ways to solve problems. It helps employees to feel as though they are valued members of the team...working together as a true team...helping create that "third mind" and coming up with a fresh approach that hadn't been thought of before.

Empowering employees can be huge morale booster. Not only does it help them to genuinely feel a part of the team and like they are making a difference to the organization...the organization also benefits from ideas that come from employees deeper in the organization that aren't usually able to express their ideas.

Multi Location Groups – If the organization is large enough to have employees in several locations, it can be valuable to have several employees from different locations in one group. Think "vertical mastermind group" over the phone with a mastermind coach to lead the group. Hearing how other people in the organization have done things in different parts of the country may bring new ways of thinking to other areas.

Mastermind groups can work with large or small companies of ANY type of industry. There is no industry that can't benefit from a mastermind group.

TOBY AND ANDREA: Of course both Toby and Andrea both have small businesses that can benefit from the mastermind group. While Toby has a few employees, Andrea has just herself.

What kind of organization do you have and how will a Mastermind group fit in to that organization?

Your Notes:

"Life is not simply holding a good hand. Life is playing a poor hand well......"

By Unknown

Chapter 9 - How Do I Find a Mastermind Group to Join?

"Let us not be content to wait and see what will happen, but give us the determination to make the right things happen."

- Peter Marshall

By now you're probably convinced...you want to join a mastermind group...you just don't know how to find one to join!! Here are the steps on how to find a mastermind group to join:

1. **Where to look –** This is most definitely the toughest part! It really starts with a question before this one and that is:

   a. **What are you looking for?** You need to know your goal first. Otherwise you'll be searching and searching and won't know it when it's right in front of you. Do you want a mastermind group that focuses on salesmanship? On Internet marketing? On first-year businesses? On woman-owned businesses? You may have two or three types of groups that you are interested in – that's okay. You may need to be a little flexible in case you don't find one group that meets all your needs; you might find another that does. But know, in general, what you are looking for.

   b. **Ask your circle of friends –** It's amazing how many people are aware of things that you don't know about! Simply asking friends and acquaintances if they know of a good mastermind group may lead you to a resource right away. You don't know if you don't ask.

c. **Meetup.com** – Meetup is a fantastic place to look for others who have the same interests as you. Do a search for something as general as "prior military" or as specific as "Denver Internet marketers" and you'll find meetup groups that fit the profile! There are meetings held in your area and they are a great place to network and find out about mastermind groups on the topic.

d. **Craigslist** – Another great place to find other people with your same interest – post an ad looking for mastermind groups.

e. **Google** – Always your friend! You'll find plenty of information about online mastermind groups. Do a broad or specialized search and you can sift through the material to find an online mastermind group.

f. **Forums** – Go to any forums or blogs that you frequent and ask for referrals of mastermind groups that people have found to be useful. Be prepared. You will probably hear some negative comments about mastermind groups, too. It just means they weren't in a well-run group!

g. **Facebook** – Ask your friends and acquaintances on Facebook for a referral. You can also do a search for Fan pages of Mastermind groups for referrals.

h. **LinkedIn** – My favourite business social networking site! You can post a note on your LinkedIn wall, ask some of your contacts, or do a search on mastermind groups in the group search and see what you come up with. If you are a member of any group on LinkedIn (and you SHOULD BE!) post a message in the group to see if anyone has a good referral. It's a business networking site – use it!

Once you've found several different groups that look like they might be promising, it's time to dig in a little further…

   2. What can I contribute? – Please note that this question is coming before number 3. It is important that YOU be able to contribute something to the group. You will feel like a fish out of water very quickly if you are always silent because you have nothing to contribute to the group. That is not what a mastermind group is about. You don't (and should NEVER) have to feel like you are a "teacher" in the group. You just want to feel like you have something of worth to contribute on a regular basis: experience, insight, thoughts or ideas.

3. How can the group help me? – At the same time, you want to be sure that you are "being fed". It is equally frustrating to feel as though you are contributing each time the group meets and are never getting anything out of the group. Make sure that as you look over the group summary you feel as though there is something you will get out of the group. Of course you will never know for sure until you actually start meeting with the group. But you should have a pretty good feeling at least.

4. How is it structured? – Pay careful attention to how the mastermind group is structured – and that there IS structure. A GIANT red flag would be something to the effect of: "We're not a mastermind group that believes in stuffy rules!"

While it may seem enjoyable and social at first to have a group that gets together and talks for an hour or two, whether it be on the phone or at lunch…when nothing is being accomplished, the group with fall apart quickly.

There are different ways to structure mastermind groups, but the two important things to note are that 1) There is structure, and 2) You like the structure the group has.

5. Is there a set number of members? Some groups will let an unlimited number of members attend, while others have a set number and they then put any additional people on a waiting list. If a member leaves the group, they will then call the next person on the waiting list to see if they want to join.

Personally, I prefer keeping the groups at a limited number. I think going to a large number lets the group get out of hand. Keeping the number small allows for more of an intimate group environment. The trust can build up quicker. I also find that the groups tend to be "stickier". They are a closer group and stay together longer when they are a smaller, more exclusive group. I find that 8 to 12 members are about the "prime" number.

6. **What is the process for joining?** This is kind of an interesting question! Do they just let "anyone" in? Or do they have you come to one of the mastermind meetings first and see if you and they think it's a good fit? Or is there a "get to know you" call to see if there is a good fit? Each group will have their own way of operating. And you'll have to decide what you are comfortable with as well. You'll know if it feels good and right!

After you've done your due diligence, you've hopefully found the mastermind group that's right for you!! If you get into it for a few weeks or months and it just isn't working…that's okay! You're not married to the group. You can leave the group and join a different one. OR…you can decide to start your own mastermind group if you think you have a different direction you want to go.

TOBY: *Toby made the decision to start doing some research to find a mastermind group that he could join. He knew that he wanted to find a group in his local area that consisted of others businesses. He didn't care what kind of businesses they were. He actually hoped that they would be a variety of types, but he was open to possibilities.*

Most of his friends were from his high school days and from the soccer club. He asked a few people, but no one really knew of anything. He checked with the local Chamber of Commerce and they didn't know what he was even talking about. He didn't think his Facebook friends would get him much further. He was wondering if he was going to be able to find a group in his area.

Next Toby went to meetup.com. He did a search for mastermind groups in his area. He found a few different groups. WHEW! Now the question was which one to think about actually joining. He looked at the profiles of the groups. He eliminated two immediately because it looked like they met pretty infrequently. It seemed like both had a very loose structure. That's not what he was looking for.

There was one that was made up of all doctors. Obviously that was a vertical group that wasn't a good fit for him. There were two more that looked like possibilities. Both met on a regular basis and looked like they had a strong agenda. Not only did they meet regularly, but they also had comments that were posted on the meetup.com board, so Toby could tell they were very active.

There was one key difference between the groups though. One had a group size of 20 or so people. It was more of a "networking group" than a mastermind group. The other had 8 people in it and seemed much more like a true mastermind group.

Toby called the number on the meetup.com page and talked to one of the members. He found out that they had two more spots that were available. The group consisted of mostly small business owners, although there was one member that was an executive from a large company in the area. The group had been meeting for about 8 months consistently. After talking to Toby extensively about his background and what he wanted to get out of the mastermind group, the member invited Toby to come to a session to see if he and they thought it would be a good fit.

Toby did go to the next session. The group seemed like a good fit for him. Of course the first time he was a little quiet, but did have a few things to add. It gave him a much better idea of what a mastermind group is, and what he would gain from it. He and the members decided he would join.

ANDREA: *Andrea was not as fortunate. She went to LinkedIn first to try to find a mastermind group, but all the ones she found were either full, or for a specific type of internet marketer that she was not. For instance one group was for people who had made £1 million or more, another one was for affiliate marketers, and another was for internet marketers who had been in business for at least one year.*

Next Andrea turned to the forums. Still no luck. She found other people who were LOOKING for mastermind groups, but not another mastermind group that met her needs to join. She didn't want to try meetup.com because she really wasn't interested in meeting locally with a group. She did put a note on her Facebook page, but didn't get any replies with the exception of people wanting to know what a mastermind group was.

Andrea is a little bit frustrated. She really wants to be in a mastermind group. She knows the value. She's just not sure what to do next.

Start researching options for mastermind groups.

What do you come up with?

Your Notes:

> *"I have seen and witnessed more people defeated by themselves than by their competitors"*
>
> — Moe Nawaz

Chapter 10 - How Do I Start a Mastermind Group?

"The best way to predict the future is to create it".

- Peter Drucker

As we talked about in Chapter 9, there are many possibilities for you to find a mastermind group to join. You may join one, stay for awhile and find that it doesn't quite fit your needs, then try another and find it doesn't either. Or you may have some trouble finding a good one right from the beginning. That doesn't mean mastermind groups don't work for you...it just means you haven't found a good one yet! If you want to avoid the frustration of going in and out of "trying out" different groups, you have another option...start one of your own!

This gives you the option to have a little more control. You will have more of a say in the people who come in to the group, and you'll have much more of a say in how the group is run. You don't necessarily have to be the mastermind coach. You can put together the group, but find someone else that you think would be a better coach to actually facilitate the sessions. However, the format of the group can still be yours! Here are the basics of how you would go about staring your own mastermind group:

1. **Decide on the Focus or Purpose of Your Mastermind Group** – In order to attract members, and to have a successful group, you will need to have an overall focus or purpose for your

group. Are you looking for online marketers? Business owners in any niche? Or in a particular niche? Women network marketers? What do you want to accomplish? General business and revenue building ideas? Lead-generating mastermind group only within your niche? You can be general or specific, but you must know your focus or purpose. You should be able to clearly state it to anyone you talk to about joining the mastermind group. By stating the focus or purpose, someone should know if it fits their needs or not.

2. **Decide on how many people you want in the Mastermind Group** – We've talked about this in previous chapters. I believe that the minimum is four in order to have a group that is engaging and involved. I like to keep the group at a minimum of around eight, but absolutely no more than twelve. You want to be sure that you have plenty of time to give to everyone. You also want to be sure that there is enough time that everyone gets to know each other. A large part of the group growing and really connecting is building trust, and that is hard to do if the group is too large. It's up to you how many people you want in your group, but decide on a number and don't go over it!

3. **Decide on a time and date you will meet** – Much of this will be dependent on the type of group you are looking to form. If it's made up of professionals who have traditional work office jobs, you'll need to meet after work hours, during the week, or on the weekend. Weekends can be tricky. I suggest early on a Saturday so people can still have the rest of their weekend if you really want to have it on the weekend. Otherwise weeknights tend to work far better. If your group type tends to have more flexibility, you can try during the work week or evenings after work.

You may have a type of group that you have decided to meet over the phone. That can work, too! Many online marketers have no problem meeting during the day over the phone. Again, you will be a good judge based on YOUR timeframe. You are looking for people similar to you. (In a way!)

Plan on always meeting at the same time. Some groups meet every two weeks. Others meet once a month. This is your group; you get to decide. Ninety minutes tends to be the best time to set aside for a mastermind group. If people want to socialize longer, they are welcome to, but 90 minutes of solid mastermind time is good. In my own groups we have a rule of a minimum of 4 hours but if workshops are needed then we turn them into a full day and a full weekend if needed as well.

4. **Find a location** – If it's over the phone – you are done! If you are going to hold the meetings in person, you'll need to find a good location that is neutral and conducive to talking. A loud restaurant will NOT do. If it's a restaurant with a closed off back room that is private, that can work, as long as the members are willing to buy a meal (if that's what is required). Take a look at other facilities such as churches, libraries (many have private rooms), colleges, or meeting or conference rooms at some office buildings (check out your local Chamber of Commerce). Make sure you find a location that you'll be able to meet at consistently for at least twelve months at a time.

5. **Set an agenda** – Now the important stuff! It is very important that you decide what your agenda is going to be BEFORE you start talking to potential members. You want them to know that you have taken the time to think this through and are going to take it seriously. This is not a social session. This is a business mastermind session that has a purpose and will be a valuable addition to their business and personal growth. You can set the agenda however you want. Here is a suggested agenda that you may want to use:

A. Welcome

B. Round Robin – Check in on goal(s) from last session – "How Did you Do?"

C. HOT SEAT – Each person has 15-20 minutes with their "Question of the Night" – All other members go around and give their input/insight, one-by-one in that timeframe.

D. CELEBRATIONS – Each member gives a celebration.

E. GOAL SETTING – Each gives a goal they want to accomplish by next session

Alternative

An alternative to Hot Seat would be A Topic of the Night. A topic would have been chosen at the previous session. Each member has 10-15 minutes to give their thoughts and ideas. A new Topic is picked before everyone leaves that night.

Whatever agenda you set, have it in writing to give to your potential members when you talk to them. You can always amend it based on input from the group after the first meeting or two, but least you have a starting point!

6. **Start Finding Members** – We'll go into this in more detail in Chapter 11, but it's time to start finding members for your mastermind group! You'll want to post ads on Craigslist, on Facebook, Gumtree, and in places where your "type" of mastermind people would be hanging out! Talk to friends, acquaintances, anyone who knows of business people that you would like to have in your mastermind group. You need to let people know that you have a mastermind group and are looking for the right individuals to join!

7. **Setting Guidelines** – It is best to have a set of guidelines that the members are aware of right from the beginning. They can be amended if agreed on by all the members, but you want to be sure that any members that join are willing to abide by the guidelines.

Guidelines would lay out policies such as confidentiality, respectfulness and attendance requirements. Here is an example of a guideline.

Sample Guidelines for a Mastermind Group

Each MasterMind group member agrees to follow these guidelines:

1. The group shall be made up with a minimum of four and maximum of twelve people who agree that the major purpose of the group is mutual growth of mind and spirit in an atmosphere

of total trust. Group members should be from different industries to achieve maximum effectiveness.

2. Our primary motivations for creating this ongoing group are to set personal and / or professional goals to increase profits for 2013 support and hold each other accountable for action towards achieving those goals.

3. Group members will avoid discussing controversial topics such as politics, religion or any other subject that is touchy. Never introduce any subject that will weaken the cordial and cooperative spirit of the group. In order to maintain trust and confidence between members of the group, all discussions must be treated as confidential.

4. The group will meet every two weeks for two hours.

5. Group members will treat each other with respect and will not interrupt each other when one member is speaking.

6. New members may be added to the group only with the unanimous consent of all members of the group. All new memberships must be on a trial basis to ensure harmony with the others. The group shall not exceed twelve members.

7. The group will be led by a professional coach. If the current coach is no longer amenable to the group, a new coach will be chosen by unanimous consent of all members of the group. The new coach must be on a trial basis to ensure harmony with the group.

8. The Master Mind Principle espouses, "No two minds ever come together without synergy, thereby creating a third invisible force which may be likened to a third mind." This third, invisible force is often called a "cosmic consciousness" or a "Master Mind." (See Napoleon Hill's *Think and Grow Rich*)

9. Attendance at every meeting is mandatory in order to keep the group viable and functioning as a mastermind. If you do not attend two meetings in a row, you will be removed from the group unless you advise the coach within 48 hours that you will not be attending.

10. A mastermind group must work with a definite plan. Read and reread Napoleon Hill's *Think and Grow Rich*, and put the power of your mind to work for you!

8. **Start Meeting!** Simple as that! Take a leap of faith and start meeting. The first meeting may not go as smooth as silk, but it will be a start. And it will probably go much better than you expect! It will be a purpose YOU have chosen, with an agenda YOU wanted, and people YOU have approved. HURRAY! Everything else can be smoothed out from there! In upcoming chapters we'll be talking about how to make your mastermind group the BEST it can be! For now, just enjoy the fact that you have created a group!

Don't look to perfect the group, the members the agenda and so on, because you will never get it off the floor. I have seen too many people who say I am not quite ready yet but soon, I will be. As Michael Masterson the bestselling author of **"Ready Fire Aim"** says get it out the door then you can always fine tune it, no matter what it is you are trying to do, JUST DO IT.

Just like this book, I have to do two version of this book one for the UK market and one for the American market both need spelling changing to meet the market needs, and is it £ or $. A number of factors have to be taken into account, but I am not going sit and wait till everything is ready, which could take forever. All I know is, I have to get my first 10,000 out in print and on the book shelves and on Amazon by November 2011. Then change whatever I need in the next print run.

ANDREA: *After Andrea's frustration with not finding a solid fit for a mastermind group to join, she decided to start one herself. Here are the things she decided on:*

1. **Purpose or focus** – A group of internet marketers who want to grow their business. The group can have internet marketers from a variety of niches and she would prefer to have them from a variety of experience levels.

2. **Number of people** – Andrea decided she wanted a minimum of five people to start the mastermind group and get it off the ground. She wants to cap the group at ten people.

3. **Time and date** – This will be subject to change depending on the people that join the group and what works for the majority. However, Andrea knows that the group will meet every two weeks for 90 minutes. As she is setting up the group, she is letting them know that it will be tentatively set for Tuesday nights at 7:00pm EST.

4. **Location** – The meetings will be held on the phone via GoToWebinar. This way if someone wants to share their screen or show something via PowerPoint, they can do so. Also, the calls can be recorded if someone in the group wants to go back and listen to them again.

5. **Agenda** – Andrea feels she needs to have at least an outline of what the agenda will be as she starts talking to potential members of the group. The agenda can always be changed later if the group as a whole decides to tweak it a bit. But for now, she is going to let them know the agenda will be:

A. *Welcome/Introductions*

B. *Round Robin – Check in on goal(s) from last session – "How Did You Do?"*

C. *Topic of the Night – A topic chosen regarding internet marketing that one member will choose the previous session – each member will have 10-15 minutes to give insights/thoughts/ideas.*

D. *CELEBRATIONS – Each member gives a celebration*

E. *GOAL SETTING – Each gives a goal they want to accomplish by next session*

6. **Finding members** – *Andrea started by posting on some of her LinkedIn groups and her Facebook page that she was starting a mastermind group for internet marketers. She also went back to some of the forums where she had looked for groups, but had other people LOOKING for mastermind groups and put some posts as well.*

7. **Setting guidelines** – *Andrea decided to wait until the first meeting and set the guidelines together as a group. Although she was putting the group together, she really wants the guidelines to be a group effort. She has some things in mind, but as she was talking to people about joining, she has asked them to bring any thoughts as to guidelines to the first "meeting".*

Would you consider starting your own mastermind group?

If so, how would you go about doing it?

Your Notes:

*"Handicaps can only
disable us if we let them.
This is true not only of
physical challenges,
but of emotional and
intellectual ones as well…
I believe that real and lasting
limitations are created in
our minds, not our bodies"*

- Roger Crawford

Chapter 11 - Who Should I Invite Into My Mastermind Group?

"A little group of wise hearts is better than a wilderness of fools."

– **John Ruskin**

In Chapter 10 we discussed setting up your own mastermind group. Deciding where to have the group and what the guidelines and agenda should be are the easy parts. The hardest part comes down to…."Who should I invite into my mastermind group?!?!"

Really, it's the people that make or break the group, right? You don't want someone who sits at the back of the room and doesn't offer anything to the group. Yet you also don't want a loudmouth who offers their opinion and doesn't let anyone else get a word in. Isn't that what you're really afraid of? Getting that "perfect mix?"

Well, I hate to burst your bubble, but there is no perfect mix! The beauty of this world is there is a crazy mix of personalities. You never know how five to twelve personalities are going to interact with each other. You could take two of those people, mix them in with another three or four people, and those original two may act completely differently in the new mix.

But again, that is the beauty of the mastermind! You never know what you're going to get! Incredible ideas come out of these groups of minds like you can't believe. And a group that doesn't seem to produce anything special one meeting can really connect and produce something spectacular the very next meeting!

So while there is no "perfect mix," there are some things that you do want to be looking for.

1. **Do They Meet Your Focus /Purpose of the Group?** – As we discussed in the previous chapter, when you state your focus or purpose of the mastermind group, can they say, "Yes, that is something that fits me"? If yes, that is someone who may be worth inviting. If not, you would NOT want to invite them.

2. **Are They Committed to Coming to the Meetings?** - A mastermind group does NOT work with members who just "drop in" here and there. As I've mentioned before, it's hard for the other members to build trust with them. Members will be sharing confidential business information. If they feel like a member is untrustworthy or flighty, you will feel the trust literally sucked out of the room. Members will hold back and the group will suffer as a whole. If someone is not committed to coming to the majority of the meetings, they should not be extended an invitation.

3. **Mutually Beneficial** – Each member of the group should have something to give, as well as be able to receive, from the group. It doesn't feel good or right if there is a member in the group that seems to be taking and taking – yet never has any input or value to give. Likewise, it doesn't feel good to have a member who is always pontificating and giving advice over and over…yet never asks or feels like the group has anything to offer. Maybe the group doesn't. If not, they really shouldn't be in that group – another group would fit their needs much more. Before you extend an offer, make sure you feel that a potential member would have something to offer the group AND would be able to benefit from the group as well.

4. **Similar Experience Levels** – I would say probably one of the reasons I see people quit mastermind group most frequently is when they feel there is a large disparity with experience levels within the group. Group members like to be able to talk and bounce ideas around with others who either 1) are going through the beginner frustrations…just like them or 2) have "been there, done that"…just like them. It's usually the people with a higher experience level that get very frustrated when they

feel like they don't have someone with experience to talk to in a group of newbie's. They tend to feel like they are there just to have their brains picked. It may feel good to be put on a pedestal at first, but they quickly get frustrated and end up leaving the group.

This can be solved by making sure you invite group members with similar experience levels. They don't have to be exact…but try not to have a large disparity. It can be either experience levels or success levels that you base this criteria on, but it's important to have a baseline and not mix it up too much.

Once you've decided who to invite…start inviting! AND start asking for referrals. It may not be the right time for someone right now…but they may have a business acquaintance that they know it will be the perfect timing for.

ANDREA: *Andrea had quite the experience as she started talking to people about joining the mastermind group. The first thing she realized is that she made a mistake in assuming that people understood what a mastermind group was. She found that many people assumed that it was either 1) a networking group or 2) a training group/opportunity. Many other of the "10 Myths of the Mastermind Group" that were discussed in Chapter 4 came in to play.*

Andrea realized that she needed an interview sheet of shorts. One that she could run through and ask each person a set of questions that would help her determine if the person might be a good fit for the group.

Of course, there are other intangibles as well! Sometimes, it just doesn't "feel right"...and that's okay! When you are the one putting the group together, you have the luxury of not inviting a person that doesn't feel right!

Andrea developed this list of questions to interview her potential mastermind group members:

1. *Are you familiar with what a mastermind group is/does?*
2. *Can you tell me a little about your business? What do you do? How long have you been in business?*
3. *What would you like to achieve by being a member of this mastermind group?*
4. *What do you think you could best contribute to the group?*
5. *What would be your commitment level to the group?*
6. *Are you prepared to participate at every meeting?*
7. *Do you have any questions for me?*

Andrea found as she asked these questions, she was able to weed out quite a few people. There were some who stated that they were very busy and could only attend meetings every once in a while. That just won't work. It's too hard to establish trust and camaraderie when members are there intermittently. There were some people who stated that they really were very shy and didn't feel that they could offer anything, but would be more than willing to listen. Again, that is not what a mastermind group is about! It's about full out participation, not just receiving great ideas!

Andrea spent a lot of time talking and emailing with potential members of the mastermind group. She had her list narrowed down to about 15 people, but knew that was still too many. She knew she needed to still narrow the list down a bit more. Our next chapter will give her some help in how to do that.

Mastermind Groups

Think about inviting people to a mastermind group that you are starting.

How would YOU go about finding people?

Would you come up with a list of questions?

How might they differ from Andrea's?

Your Notes:

*"No business can exist
For itself alone.
It must provide some
products or services to
the needs or wants,
of others; or it will
cease to be profitable
therefore leading
to bankruptcy"*

- Moe Nawaz

Chapter 12 - Qualities of the People in Successful Mastermind Groups

Once you have invited people in to your group – you want to take a look at the people and ask yourself…are these the RIGHT people for my group? To answer that question, I'm going to give you some insight in my experience of years as a Mastermind Coach. I'm going to share with you the top qualities of people in SUCCESSFUL mastermind groups. I consider these to be similar qualities in people that help make the groups successful.

- **COMMITTED** – They are committed to their group and committed to the other members. They show up on time meeting after meeting. They take being in their mastermind group very seriously. If they can't make the group meeting for some reason, they let the group members know ahead of time.

They consider the mastermind group to be a key component to the success of their business. Therefore, they are prepared when they come to the mastermind group meetings with any "homework" done. They also are thinking of the mastermind group in between sessions and storing away ideas that could be helpful to different members.

- **PROBLEM SOLVERS** - You never hear a "Gee, I don't know," out of a successful mastermind group. The people in the group start digging in and throwing out ideas. They have unique ideas and solutions to unique problems and aren't afraid to bring any idea to the table.

A good problem solver is someone who listens, asks questions and then makes a suggestion. Based on the feedback that is given by the other members, they continue through the same process.

- **DIVERSE** – The group as a whole is diverse. It's no fun to have a bunch of cookie cutters all agreeing or thinking of the exact same solution! Having diverse ideas and thoughts leads to very unique solutions.

Diverse-thinking individuals are also important. A person should be willing to look at things from diverse angles. If they ONLY ever look at things from one side, they tend to not be a good fit in to a mastermind group. You will find the group getting "stuck" when it comes to that person.

- **RESPECTFUL** – You want members that are very respectful of one another. They let each other express their ideas fully, no matter how "out there" they may be. They may ask for clarification if they don't understand but would never scoff or say, "You're crazy." Every idea and thought is respected.

Believe me, you WILL hear some pretty "wild and crazy" ideas sometimes. There is a way to laugh and have fun with someone, but still be respectful.

You also want people who will be respectful enough to give each person their time to speak. No interrupting when someone else has the floor. There are people who like to be "floor hogs" and speak ALL THE TIME. They think that their opinions are more important than anyone else's. There may be a group that is a good fit for them, but a mastermind group typically is not. Everyone should be respectful of each other's time, thoughts and energy in the group.

- **OPEN** – They are open in speaking their thoughts and minds and open to hearing other people's thoughts. It's a two-way street. There are no pre-conceived notions coming in to any meeting. Dale Carnegie taught that one of the top qualities that any person can bring to a mastermind group is a positive mental attitude...that is being open at its very best!

It can take a few meetings to get everyone to open up. Some people have the ability to just "let go" right away and let everything out. Others take more time to build up trust before they can be fully open. But they must be open to hearing everyone's thoughts. They should never shut anyone down. All ideas are worthy. And eventually, they should be equally open to sharing their ideas.

I'm sure you can tell that I highly value the members of the mastermind groups I have had. They have to highly value each other as well. It seems that those who "don't fit" tend to leave on their own. It's funny how that happens!

I can also tell you that the people who "don't fit" do have some similar qualities as well. I think it's important to take a little time to discuss those people. Here are some qualities that don't do well in a mastermind group:

KNOW IT ALL – The person who want to monopolize every conversation because they have "been there, done that"…for EVERYTHING. You sometimes wonder if they've lived nine lives. The problem isn't that they want to share their experience. The problem gets to be when they aren't letting other people share THEIR experiences because they are monopolizing the time and conversation (or at least trying to…hopefully you have a good mastermind coach stepping in!). They tend to be people who are negative, selfish, critical and demanding. Those types of people will destroy a mastermind group and should be dismissed from a group as soon as possible.

CYNICAL - We've talked about the mastermind groups being a positive environment. That is what they should be. Now that doesn't mean that it has to be roses and rainbows all the time. Everyone can certainly bring up the "other side" of the situation, play devil's advocate, etc. But if you a person that is constantly "the cynic," it wears down on the group. You'll see the group visibly tense when it comes time for that person to speak. That is not positive for the group.

YES PERSON – It's also not productive to have a person who just agrees with what every person says. In other words, they lack their own opinion and just agree with everyone else's opinion. They may be getting great information for their own business, but remember, this is a two-way street. The rest of the group will eventually just tune this person out if they recognize that they never add anything of unique value to the conversations.

FUNNY GUY – Yes, it's great to have a little fun with business! Of course things don't have to be stuffy. But the constant jokester can get old after a while if they are NEVER taking things seriously, and it does happen.

TOO TECHIE TO PAY ATTENTION – If you have an **in-person** mastermind group, you'll know this person right away. They pop open their laptop and have their smart phone open and going at the same time. Their eyes are darting from the person talking, to their phone or computer screen, and it doesn't take but about ten minutes before their fingers start flying. It's rude and distracting. You can hear them on the phone too…typing away…or their Skype dinging while the mastermind call is going on. There should be a strict "all electronics off" rule during mastermind calls (unless someone is expecting their wife to go into labour). If that can't be a rule for some reason, and people can't pay attention, they should be asked to leave the group.

Again, if someone doesn't fit and doesn't leave on their own accord, they need to be asked to leave. The mastermind group needs to be a cohesive positive group!

TOBY: Toby attended his first mastermind meeting in his area. It consisted of nine other business members. The meeting was 90 minutes long with a pretty well laid out agenda. Looking over the items above for what qualities in the people of the group make for a successful mastermind group, here is what Toby found:

COMMITTED: He was impressed with the commitment level of the members in the group. He could tell from the conversations that they had a strong relationship with one another and the trust factor was high. One of the members mentioned how sorry he was that he would be on vacation and would miss the next session, but made arrangements to call one of the other members to see what happened and if there was any "homework" or what the hot seat topic would be for the next session so he could be prepared.

PROBLEM SOLVERS: Again, Toby was very impressed. These guys (and one gal) were not afraid to dig in and help each other work on issues in each other's businesses. They asked tough personal questions, and they gave honest answers that helped the others to dig deeper. There was some real progress made during the session.

DIVERSE: The group was fairly diverse. There were varying ages and experience levels within the group. With that came some very diverse ways at looking at problems! It was interesting to see how different business people looked at an issue. Toby's mind was really opened up to seeing the possibilities of what the mastermind might be able to do for his business.

RESPECTFUL: This was another area that was impressive to Toby. When he was around his large family of in-laws and business did come up, he was used to everyone talking over each other. It was always hard to get a word in edgewise. Many times he ended up just sitting back and letting everyone else give their opinion – it just wasn't worth fighting for talking time.

At the mastermind group everyone was very respectful of each other's time to talk AND what each other had to say. Each person had the group's full attention when they talked. They were asked questions, and they had the time to answer. New concept to Toby. When one person DID interrupt, someone else in the group jokingly (but firmly) put him in his place.

OPEN: Everyone in the group was certainly open. No one had trouble speaking their mind or listening to any idea that anyone else had to say.

Overall, the whole experience was eye-opening and exciting to Toby. He was very enthusiastic about the prospect of what the mastermind group could mean for his business. The group seemed like a GREAT fit. After the session he met with the facilitator who agreed that Toby could join the group.

ANDREA: *As Andrea had her list of 15 people that she had narrowed her list down to, she knew that she needed to narrow the list down a bit more. She really was having a hard time deciding on how to do this. She knew that she could call them each back and ask them something like how to rate themselves on each of the above qualities, but would that REALLY give her a good feeling for how they would fit in the group?*

After giving it much thought, Andrea decided to hold a "preview mastermind call". She let each of the 15 people know that the call was a two-fold process. First, to see if the mastermind call was something that THEY really felt comfortable being a part of and second, to see if they were a good fit for the group.

She knew that it wouldn't be a FULL mastermind call. She scheduled it for 90 minutes and told each person that they would simply be doing an introduction of the call, and then give each person five minutes to introduce themselves and tell the others what they would like to achieve from the mastermind group. Each person would only have five minutes. At the end of the call there would be ten minutes for general questions.

The one quality that Andrea knew she probably wouldn't be able to get a good gauge on would be problem solving, but she felt the other qualities would come out well enough to get a better sense of how the people reacted in a mastermind group setting. Here is how things played out:

COMMITMENT: *One person didn't show up to the call at all. They were out! Another person showed up 15 minutes late. Andrea realized that this was a red flag and made a note that if they didn't let her know after the call why (and it was a really good reason) they would also be out. They did not contact her after the call. Everyone else seemed very committed to the idea of being in the mastermind group.*

DIVERSE: *Overall the group seemed very diverse. They came from a variety of internet marketing backgrounds. Some were newer; some more experienced.*

RESPECTFUL: Almost everyone was respectful. There was one "floor hog". The time was set at five minutes for each person, and everyone was cognizant of their time expect for one person. He was at seven minutes when Andrea tried to politely let him know that it was time to wrap up...and he bowled right over her. He let her know that he had a lot to offer the group with his years of experience and should probably be the leader of the group...and he kept on talking. Andrea was able to stop him at nine minutes. She made a note that he would not be in the group.

OPEN: Everyone was very open for the first session. Obviously there was only five minutes, and it was the first session, so there was some trepidation. Not everyone shared their product or niche...some just said they were in eCommerce or had an info product. This was understandable. Internet marketing is a cut-throat business and no one wants to give away their idea or secret until they trust someone! Some people were very open and willing to share though.

At the end of the call Andrea let everyone know that if they had any questions...or felt they did not want to be a part of the group to please let her know. She also let them know she would contact everyone within a few days with the final decision on the group members.

One person immediately emailed Andrea to let her know that she did not want to be a part of the group. She felt that the experience level of some of the members was not at a high enough level to be of worth to her. Fair enough (even though you can ALWAYS learn from people at any level!! It's better not to have someone in the group if they feel this way!)

That left Andrea with four people who were out. She still had eleven and had decided to cap it at ten. Andrea went back over her notes carefully. She realized that there was one person who was very quiet. He actually only talked for 2 ½ of the five minutes and was very – flat when he talked. When she looked over the call report she realized that he actually left 30 minutes into the call. He was the last person she cut from the group. The commitment and the openness was not there.

That left Andrea with her ten. She called each of them to verify that they were still interested in being in the group. They were all very excited to join and participate. She finally had her mastermind group!!

What qualities do YOU have that will make you a good candidate for a mastermind group?

Your Notes:

> "In my life I have seen people in business, who have hesitated because of fear of feeling inferior, whilst I have seen others busy making mistakes and becoming superior"
>
> - Moe Nawaz

Chapter 13 – Key Qualities of a Mastermind Coach

"People do not care how much you know until they know how much you care."

– John Maxwell

When it comes to being in a mastermind group…whether you join one that is already in place or you put one of your own together, you will want to make sure that there is a QUALITY mastermind coach leading the group. Some groups will try to run in a much less-structured atmosphere, and we'll go into that more in our final chapter. I have some pretty strong feelings about that!

For now, I want to concentrate on some key qualities that a good mastermind coach should have. If you are not finding that the mastermind coach in your group has these qualities, your group either needs to find a new coach, or you need to look for a new group.

1. **A Great Listener** – Note that this doesn't say a good listener. Good is not enough in the listening department of mastermind coaching. A mastermind coach needs to be a **great** listener. This is a hard quality to master. First of all, if the coach has a background in business, they may want to jump in and give advice based on their experience and background.

A mastermind coach's job is to listen carefully to what is being said by the person in the hot seat, and by all the participants who are giving their input. It is often up to the coach to rephrase and clarify statements that are being misunderstood because OTHERS aren't fully listening. A mastermind coach has to be committed to being fully "in the moment" of the group at all times.

A good mastermind mind coach will often be heard saying: "So let's make sure we have this right. If I understand what you're saying..." and they will clarify the statement such as "...you are frustrated that your employees are showing up late to work almost every day. You've talked to them about it, but it's not doing any good. You want some suggestions on what to next. They are good at what they do, and you don't really want to take the time and money to train new employees, but you NEED them to be on time. Is that correct?"

At the end of the session, the mastermind coach may reiterate what the participants had to say. Such as:

"Okay, so John thought you should...."

"Natalie suggested you...."

And so on. "Is that correct?"

Again, it's clarifying to make sure everyone has heard and understands what has been said. Their job is to get everyone to "buy off" on the problems and the suggestions/solutions.

2. **Focuses on Solutions Instead of Problems** – Nothing is worse than being in a mastermind group full of whiners that don't move forward! A good mastermind coach will let the problems be heard, but will make sure that everyone is focusing on the solutions rather than the problems. It takes a lot of work, especially when you have one or two people who want to keep bringing up their problems again and again. Laser focusing on solutions is what you need in a coach.

There is no use in beating a dead horse! A good mastermind coach will say something to the effect of: "Okay Erik, we understand that you want to get more customers to your website. We know that you have tried a PPC campaign that didn't work very well. Now let's give everyone in the group time to be in the hotseat and give their input as to some ideas and suggestions on what you might want to try next".

If Erik tries to shut someone down when they are talking by saying "I already tried that," the mastermind coach will have to remind him that it is that person's time, and Erik will have his time again after the "solution hotseat" time is up. The goal is to get Erik solely concentrating on solutions instead of problems for an extended period of time!

3. **A Visionary Perspective** – You want a coach that helps push people to think out of the box. The saying may be cliché, but you don't want a mastermind group that just sits around and states the obvious. A good mastermind coach that is a visionary himself will keep asking the questions and prodding the group members to push themselves a little further…and then a little further. That's what will bring great things out of the group.

A good question for a mastermind coach is, "If there were no barriers to your problem, what would you choose to do?" Or, "What if you could do ANYTHING to change that part of your business…time and money weren't an obstacle…what would you do?" "How can you work around the obstacles to still make that work?" A good coach will make their members stretch their minds.

4. **An Enforcer of Rules** – You can't have a mastermind coach that lets the set rules slide. The established rules are there for a reason, and if the coach doesn't enforce them, your mastermind group will suffer. You want a coach that will stick to the agenda and enforce any rules that the group has decided on. Now, if the group decides that a rule needs to be changed, that is fine, but just letting rules slide will lead to a group that is not cohesive.

5. **Results Driven** – You want a coach that cares about the results of the group. You should have an established goal and common purpose as a group, and you should always be heading toward it. You should have goals each person is working on before you meet the next time, and the coach should make sure that each person is being held accountable. Seeing results individually and as a group will give the group a feeling of purpose and worthwhile.

If a member isn't doing what they say they are going to do, the coach needs to call them on it…and hold their feet to the fire the next time. It's not about making them feel bad; it's about pushing them to their goal. They will feel so much better when they are achieving their goals.

In most of my groups we set our main goals to double and triple the size of each business within 3 years. Then we set about ways how to exponentially grow their businesses to get the results.

6. **Genuine Care** – You want a coach that genuinely cares about the success of the group. You will feel and know it when it's there…and certainly when it's not!

Think of a mastermind coach as any other coach you have had in your life…whether in sports or academia. They were there to ensure you were a success. You had rules to follow, but they were meant to help you be successful. A mastermind coach is no different.

Each coach in life has their own way of doing things. Some you click with; some you do not. Some that you don't click with…others will click with. Again, you don't have to stay with a group if the coach doesn't work for you. Make sure the coach is just as good a fit as the group is!

TOBY: *Toby could tell that his mastermind coach was a top mastermind coach. There were times that Toby didn't even remember he was there, because the group was talking and discussing business topics in a formulated way. You could tell they'd been doing this for a while. The atmosphere was relaxed, yet there was still a structure to the group.*

Occasionally someone would get a little off topic…and sometimes someone would get a little long-winded. It happens. The mastermind coach would speak up and quickly get the group back on track. The group obviously respected their mastermind coach. His authority was never undermined or questioned.

There were also a few times that the group would get stuck. A topic just didn't seem to be moving anywhere. Again, the mastermind coach would speak up, ask a couple of key questions that could get the group thinking and talking again…and the time would quickly pass by as experience and suggestions started flying.

At the end of every meeting, the mastermind coach would make sure to ask each member for a goal they would be working on for the next two weeks. And at the beginning of the next session, he was sure to check on the status of that goal. The coach and the members were sure to offer plenty of encouragement…both when things went well and when they were a little off kilter.

Toby knew without a doubt that his mastermind coach genuinely cared about each of the members in the group. He KNEW their businesses and would take the time to ask about things that had happened even months before to check up on progress.

ANDREA: *Andrea had a tough decision to make. She was the one who put together the mastermind group. Should she be the mastermind group coach? With a background in education, she certainly was qualified.*

However, her concern was that she would not get as much out of the group personally and professionally if she was the mastermind coach. She felt like she really needed someone who was not a part of the group that could run the group efficiently so she could focus on being a member of the group.

This left Andrea with another decision. She could either find someone that she felt could run a mastermind group for "free" such as a friend or previous teacher colleague, or she could find a paid mastermind coach to run the group. She had not thought of charging the people in the group before previously though.

Andrea got online and did some searching for mastermind coaches. She found several who listed specifically that they met the criteria above. She read their websites and their customer testimonials carefully and narrowed the list down to 3 mastermind coaches. She called them to see if they had availability and would be willing to take on her group...and of course what their fees would be.

She connected with one particular mastermind coach that was a very good listener and had experience working with other internet marketing mastermind groups. She had done extensive mastermind group coaching over the phone and was very results- driven. It seemed like a great fit for Andrea's group.

Andrea emailed all the members in the group to let them know the cost of the mastermind coach. All but one member was fine with the cost. That brought the number of members to nine, which was fine. It left one space open should someone have a referral for another member.

When the group met for the first time, it was a winner. The coach was able to lead the group and Andrea was able to sit back and just be a member of the group. She was happy that she was able to bring the group together, but also very grateful that she could concentrate on what was best for her business...not being a mastermind group coach.

What qualities would be most important to you in a mastermind coach?

Why?

Is there anything that would be a deal breaker for you?

Your Notes:

"Develop an attitude of gratitude, and give thanks for everything that happens to you, knowing that every step forward is a step toward achieving something bigger and better than your current situation"

- Brian Tracy

Chapter 14 - How to Maximize Your Return From a Mastermind Group

"God gives every bird its food, but He does not throw it into its nest."

- J.G. Holland

What each person will get from a mastermind group will be completely up to them. It always amazes me how in one group I will hear several people rave how the mastermind group has made such a difference to their business, yet there will be another person who will say it was not a productive use of their time.

What makes the difference between the people who find it useful and those who don't? Usually what THEY decide to put in to it. The effort and the expectations…the hope even. A positive attitude truly goes far. When you expect great things, great things happen. And as the quote says at the beginning of the chapter…you have to work a little for your food!

Here are some things that I have found through my years of experience that have been helpful for members of mastermind groups…to maximize their return from a mastermind group.

Have An Open Mind

As I've already mentioned, you need to go into the mastermind group with an open mind. Be open to other people's thoughts and opinions. Be open to other people's struggles as well. Just because something was easy for you doesn't mean it wasn't a struggle for someone else. I see people shut down by having an "Oh, are you kidding me?!? How can they think that is an issue?" attitude. It shuts down being able to have an overall open mind and doesn't allow for overall open communication within the group.

Remember, your goal is to both give and receive. In order to do both effectively you have to have an open mind in both areas. So what do you do when someone says something that you think is utterly ridiculous? It's bound to happen at one time or another. First…remember the old adage, "If you don't have anything nice to say, don't say anything at all." Translation: "If something rude is going to come out of your mouth, keep it firmly shut."

Next, take a deep breath. Close your eyes for just a moment (without rolling them). Think for just a moment. This may not be a problem for you. This may have NEVER been a problem or an issue for you. But it IS an issue for the person that is talking. To them, it's important. So just pretend like it's important to your business, too. What would you do? Talk in a voice that is not condescending – and give some insight.

Sharing Success Stories – and Failures!

This may sound easy as first glance. Some people have no problem sharing stories. Others have a little more of a difficult time opening up. It is vital that you share your success stories…and your failures…with the group. This can be stories that have happened in the past and you have learned from (good or bad) that can help other members in their particular struggle. You probably have heard your parents say, "Don't make the same mistakes I made!" You may have dismissed that instruction, but I bet you could dish out some advice to business owners that could save them time and money avoiding some of the mistakes you made early on…or even later on!

Equally important is to share a success story each week. It's a great way to either start or end the meeting. It's easy to get bogged down in what things you need help with, but it's also important to focus on what's going great! Not only does it feel good for you, but it's good energy for the group to see positive things happening as a whole to the members in the group. Especially when someone has been struggling with a particular issue and then has a break through. Celebrate that as a group! Give every person a chance to share a success story. If you have to stretch to find something to celebrate...well, stretch! If it was a really bad week and you are just celebrating the fact that you made it to the mastermind group when all you wanted to do was hide under the covers, that's okay, too!

Questions to Ask The Group

Sometime it happens...there are lulls in the conversation or a point where the group just has a pause. It's always good to have a "hip pocket" group of questions that you can ask of the members to get things going again. Here are a few that can always get the conversation going:

1. **What Is the Most Important Thing You Are Working On Right Now?** It gets each member focused on the most important thing in their business at the moment.

2. **What's the One Question...That If You Could Get the Answer To...Would Make the Biggest Difference In Your Business?** This is a great twist on asking for help from the group. It makes the members think a little deeper about a question of importance that is truly relevant to their business. The nice thing is...this changes! You can ask it again in three months and get a totally different answer from the members! I do this at most of my mastermind group meetings to stay on top of each member and what they are doing.

Go around the room and have everyone ask their question. Then go back around the room. Start with the first question and have everyone give their answer to the first question. Move on the second question and so on. Keep any unanswered questions for future sessions.

3. **Hot Seat Volunteer** – With a twist. Often times a hot seat is a member asking a question that gets round-robined with the other

members. Ask for a volunteer with a twist. The volunteer gets in a hot seat with these rules:

1. Each member gets to ask them one question about their business.
2. Go around again and each member can ask a clarifying or another question about any other question that was asked.
3. Each member then offers advice based on the previous two rounds.

You'll find that the hot seat volunteer will typically have some major break troughs in their business. Make sure that they have a follow up list of which items they intend to implement in to their business. It can be tough, but it's also very rewarding. You'll often see someone new volunteer, due to the impact on the last volunteer's business.

Keep Your Finger on the Pulse

It's very important to keep your finger on the pulse of the group. Is it meeting everyone's needs? I suggest doing a survey at least quarterly. Ask each member the following:

1. On a scale of one to ten – one being low and ten being high – How would you say the group is meeting your needs?
2. What would we need to do differently to make it a ten?
3. What do you like?
4. What would you like to see changed?

Remember that ultimately the group is about meeting the needs of…the group!

TOBY: Toby is about 4 months into his mastermind group now. He has attended on a regular basis and has only missed one session due to a soccer tournament. He has found that is has been even better than he expected...probably because he has participated more than he ever expected he would.

Toby knew that the whole idea of the mastermind group was to give as much as you take...but he still thought that he would be doing a lot more learning than he would be participating in helping other people. The whole experience has been quite a bit different then what the thought it would be.

He has realized that his 12 years of business experience really is worth something. That might sound crazy, but when you've been working by yourself, it can be hard to realize your worth at times. He's made some great contacts as well and gotten some new clients through the group – another unexpected side benefit he wasn't even looking for.

As Toby was working to build his brick and mortar store while still keep his current clientele happy, the mastermind group proved to be invaluable. The group really helped him work through some tough decisions as well as helped with some marketing ideas that have helped the store get off to a really good start.

Toby has not been afraid to share his failures or his successes along the way. Some of his past failures have been essential in helping others avoid costly mistakes. He has also been able to help some people in the mastermind group make some good connections through his own clientele.

Overall Toby would say his open mind and willingness to share are what have helped him to maximize his return from his mastermind group.

ANDREA: Andrea is also 4 months into her mastermind group. The group is running fairly well. She has been on every call they have had.

Andrea is in a slightly different position than Toby in that she constantly feels like she has to be looking out for how the group is doing as a whole...and she does! While the group is being led by a mastermind group coach, she is still the head of the group. The group looks to her for decisions on adding new members, changing any rules, etc. So while she does get to enjoy the mastermind portion, she has a few other things to watch out for as well.

Strictly a mastermind group member, Andrea is enjoying the group very much. It has been extremely good for her business. She has learned a lot from the members in the group. The experiences of the group, the ideas, and just the energy has helped her to stay focused and get the things done that she needs. She has a very open mind and is willing to share success and failure stories – she really considers herself an open book.

The mastermind coach has been great at asking questions to get the group moving along if there is ever a lull. That has not been a problem.

There have been a few members who have decided to leave, and a few new members who have joined. It's taken a little bit of time for the group to kind of "settle in". Andrea found that it was necessary to send a survey every month the first few months to keep her pulse on the group. It was a great way to make adjustments to the group to meet the needs of everyone. The time needed to be adjusted – and lengthened. Ninety minutes was just not long enough for the group of ten to be able to let everyone participate in the call. The calls are now scheduled for two hours, and people can stay on the call to socialize or ask general questions if they want to stay on longer (without the mastermind coach). There is a core group that enjoys doing that.

Now the group has settled in to include ten people. There are a total of six people from the original group. The members are finally opening up. Everyone has now shared their online business and is digging in to really help each other. Andrea feels that not only is she maximizing her return from the mastermind group…but the others in the group are as well.

How do you think you could best maximize the return from belonging to a mastermind group?

Your Notes:

"When written in Chinese, the word "crisis" is composed of two characters. One represents danger and the other represents opportunity"

– John F. Kennedy

Chapter 15 - Proactive vs. Reactive Mastermind Groups

"Always bear in mind that your own resolution to succeed is more important than any other one thing."

– Abraham Lincoln

You have the option of going with a proactive or a reactive mastermind group. The choice is up to you, and it ultimately is up to what you want and need to gain out of the mastermind group for your business.

Definition of Proactive vs. Reactive

A proactive group is a paid mastermind group. All of the members of the group have paid to be a part of the group. A paid mastermind coach is in charge of the group which is the reason the group members are paying. They are paying for the services of the professional or commercial mastermind coach.

A reactive group is a group where the members are all free members. The leader of the group can be a member of the mastermind group or another outside person who is a coach, but is not a paid coach because the members are not paying to be a part of the group.

Advantages of a Proactive Group Over a Reactive Group

There are distinct advantages of being in a proactive mastermind group. When the members are in a paid group, they tend to take the group a little more seriously. There is a REASON to make the meeting on time each time. I have found when members pay, they pay attention. The words FREE ADVICE has very little value, regardless how valuable the advice might be to people. I have learned this the hard way over the years. People who pay for the advice, learn and then put it into practice to achieve the benefits more rapidly.

You may think that simply being a part of the group is reason enough. It should be! But the fact of the matter is that people are busy. Before people start to see the value of the mastermind group, it can be the first thing they "let go of" in a busy week. Having a monetary commitment makes a person more likely to attend. The value then switches from the monetary aspect to the business aspect.

The other very distinct advantage of a proactive mastermind group is having a professional or commercial mastermind coach in charge. A professional coach has the experience of having previously led mastermind groups. They know how to get groups moving when there is a stagnant point (and it does happen). They know how to clarify points when there is confusion. They know how to set realistic goals and how to hold the group members accountable. They have the experience of what to do when a group is not meeting its goals time and time again. They know how to keep the group accountable to the rules of the group and what to do when members aren't meeting the expectations that have been set.

Having a mastermind coach that is a member of the group that does not have this experience CAN work, but it can also hold the group back as the coach learns what to do and not to do. As they have to be reactive to situations, the group can stutter and suffer.

Again, ultimately the decision is yours. Cost can be a factor for some people, and you may think that not having to pay for a mastermind group is more beneficial. But give it some closer consideration. What is REALLY better for your business? Is the trade-off of a slower ramp-up period of the mastermind group worth it? Or is it more worth having a commercial mastermind coach in charge and other members who take the group and their business seriously...and are ready to get moving forward NOW?

TOBY: When Toby joined his mastermind group, he did not realize that there was a difference between proactive and reactive groups. His particular group is a reactive group that is made up of members of the business community.

The "coach" or facilitator in his instance is a member of the group. The group has been in place for a number of years, although some members of the group have come and gone. There have been about six core members that have stayed with the group over the past four years, and the facilitator is one of them.

The facilitator in an active participant in the group. Since the group has been together for such a long period of time, it pretty much runs like a well-oiled machine. When it gets off track, the facilitator quickly reacts and gets it back on track. Although sometimes it's even some of the other members who will quickly jump in and make the adjustment.

Toby was lucky in this case. He's not sure that he would have paid to have participated in a mastermind group. He didn't fully understand the value, although he was willing to give it a go.

Toby does fully understand the value of the mastermind now, and if he were to join another mastermind group, he feels he would probably look for a proactive group led by a professional coach. He feels he DID hit the jackpot with his group this time, and wouldn't want to waste time on a group that was not led by someone who didn't know what they were doing.

ANDREA: As we know, Andrea realized early on that she was not going to be able to be both a participant and a coach in her mastermind group. She quickly saw the value in a proactive mastermind group. She hired a professional coach and it was the best thing that she could have done for the mastermind group.

Had Andrea tried to be the "coach," the ramp-up time for the mastermind group would have been much longer. She is sure that the bumpy start would have been even bumpier and they would have lost more members and had a harder time solidifying the group.

The coach was invaluable in leading the group during the awkward beginning and helping during the silences. She was great at getting conversations flowing and asking the clarifying questions. This was especially important to Andrea because as the "owner" of the group, she didn't want to *seem overly "pushy". She was doing the surveys and trying to work on some of the other administration items. She didn't want to be the one to keep asking people to speak up and talk, too!*

Andrea felt like the money that the members spent for the coach was well worth it. It also helped to keep a certain level of members in the group. While not wanting to discriminate, she also wanted people who were SERIOUS about building a business. Not just fly-by-night internet marketers. If people were willing to invest money in to a mastermind coaching session, they would have something to give to the group as well.

Not only was Andrea glad she made the decision to go with a proactive mastermind group, she would do it again in an instant.

Think carefully about the pros and cons of a proactive vs. a reactive mastermind group.

Which do you think would be a better choice for you and your business? Why?

Your Notes:

"I've come to believe that all my past failure and frustration were actually laying the foundation for the understandings that have created the new level of living am now enjoy"

– Moe Nawaz

Chapter 16 - How a Mastermind Group Can Change and Grow Your Business

"Great things are not done by impulse, but by a series of small things brought together".

- Vincent Van Gogh

The bottom line of joining a mastermind mind group is that you want to make a change to your business. And you want that change to be a positive one. The majority of the time, a business owner is looking to grow their business in size and in the amount of revenue they bring in and/or their profit.

So realistically, how can the time and effort you put in to a mastermind group change and grow your business? You should expect to see change and growth in your business in the following ways:

Accountability

As we've talked about before, when you are in business by yourself and for yourself, it's all too easy to set a goal and then let it slide a week...and then another week...and then another. If you don't accomplish your action steps to get you closer to your goal, who do you really have to be accountable to? Sure, yourself and your business. But you have the option to be easy on yourself. And believe me, a lot of people choose to do that when they don't hit their action steps or their goals. Unfortunately, what many people will do is simply stop setting goals.

How The Mastermind Changes This

When you are in the mastermind group, you have a group to be accountable to. You are setting a large goal, and setting actionable steps as goals each time you meet with your group...steps you will accomplish before you meet again. You will find that as you know you will be meeting again with your group, you WILL get your steps done. You don't want to be "the one" who doesn't get things accomplished.

It doesn't matter if that's not a great reason for getting it done! The fact of the matter is, it's propelling your business forward. It's good for you and it's good for your business.

Networking and Connecting with Success-Minded People

Can you network and connect with success-minded people without a mastermind group? Sure. But you will find that some of those relationships will be superficial, and others will be more lopsided. That is, people will expect to GET more than they will GIVE. In other connections and networking, you have no idea how success minded other people are. It's a roll of the dice.

In your mastermind group, you will know the people in your group. The group is about making connections and networking. The group will naturally introduce each other to people who will help them with their business. It is networking at its very best.

You will find that your business is changed as you make connections with success- minded people. I often say that success begets success. As you are around success- minded people, that feeling of success will rub off on you. You will see it in your attitude and confidence. That will translate into the success of your business

Change your Way of Thinking

It's been said again and again, *"You can't do the same things the same way and expect different results."* One of the things that is important to change is your way of thinking. It's not easy to change your way of thinking. After all, it's YOUR way.

The mastermind group will help you think differently. You just can't help it. You'll have other success-minded people that you'll be talking to on a regular basis, and they all have a different way of thinking. You won't think exactly like one or another, but you WILL change the way you think. That can only help your business grow.

Support

Support is another factor of being in business that can be tough when you are an entrepreneur. It can be hard not having support. Giving yourself support just doesn't cut it!

Having the support of your mastermind group can make a huge difference in your business. Knowing you have the group to turn to for support not only for your scheduled mastermind groups sessions, but in between as well (in most cases), is a huge boost. If you feel stuck or frustrated, you know you have a mastermind group session right around the corner. You'll have the group coming together that you can bring your issue to, and you'll know that they will have the synergy and ideas that will help you. With your mastermind group, you are never alone.

The "Third Mind" Phenomenon

The Third Mind is what happens when you get many minds working together. You come up with ideas that would have never been generated by anyone on their own. Your business will grow as the ideas that are generated by the third mind in your group will move your business to the next level. Not only will you benefit from the ideas generated about YOUR business…you will also benefit from the ideas that are generated about other people's businesses. That is one of the other great things about the mastermind group.

You benefit from ALL the ideas that are generated in the group, whether they are specifically about your business or not. Your business can still benefit from them.

Learning From Others' Success and Mistakes

There's another saying that goes, *"Do as I say, not as I do."* Sometimes there is definitely merit to that! You can learn from the successes and mistakes of others without having to go through all of the time and sometimes agony that others went through to learn those lessons.

You will be smart to listen closely to the success stories and the mistakes that others have made and learn from them. If you listen closely and follow the advice of others, your business will grow at a quicker rate than if you were learning all the lessons yourself.

Overall, the mastermind group and participating in it will grow and change your business at a rate that is far greater than you could ever do by yourself. Some of changes you would probably have never made, period.

Moe Nawaz: How I Run My Mastermind Groups to Transform a Business

While every coach can and does run their mastermind group differently, I'd like to share the basics of how I run my mastermind groups to help my clients transform and grow their business.

Again, keep in mind that this is how I run MY particular groups. It has been very successful for me and for my clients. Other mastermind coaches choose to run their groups differently and have differing philosophies. That's okay! You can find a group that best suits YOUR needs! However I would like to give you a taste of what I have found to work for my clients. Most of (but not all) my mastermind groups run for three years because, we set goals and targets to help them to double or triple their businesses in that three year period.

1. I run my mastermind coaching classes for a minimum of three years. The participants must commit to being a part of the group for that three year period.

2. The groups consist of maximum twelve members.

3. They meet once a month for four hours. Half of that time is spent in lectures, and the other half is Q & A's with workshops.

4. For the starting point of our mastermind group, we spend quite a bit of time working on time management. But it is based on time management in a specific and formulated way. Bear with

me as I explain this briefly (realizing that we spend several sessions on this!)

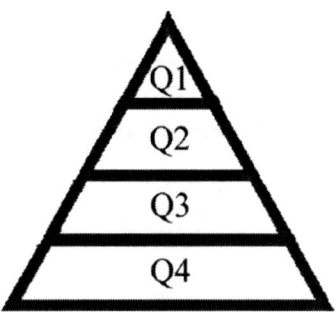

As you see here we have a triangle with FOUR separate quadrants, similar to Steven Covey. Each quadrant is represented as follows:

Q1 – The top quadrant or Q1 represents lifetime products. Those products can include information products, books, purchasing assets – anything that has a lifetime value. Once acquired, these lifetime assets generate money for life.

Q2 – The second quadrant or Q2 represents high value per hour. This is the amount of money you make per hour. High value per hour can include consultancy work or time spent creating lifetime products. This also could be targeting some major clients who take more than six months to land by directly or indirectly influencing them over a period of months well before any meeting takes place.

Q3 The third quadrant or Q3 represents low value per hour. These are the things that other people can probably do better than you. For instance it takes me three to four hours to write an article that is roughly 500 words. However, I can have a 3rd party do it and it would probably take them about 15 minutes. Spending my time writing the article would be a low value per hour item.

Q4 – The fourth quadrant or Q4 represents zero value. These are things like opening email, text messaging, booking your tee off times for golf, surfing the Internet, doodling and making social event reservations.

Now we are going to FLIP the triangle:

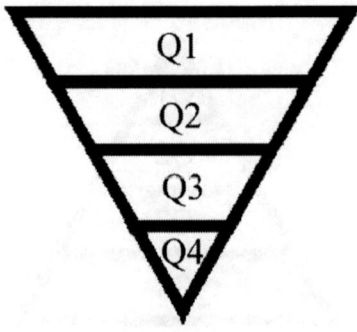

As you can see, we now have the bulk of the "time" in Q1 instead of the bulk being in Q4. The goal for the first part of our mastermind groups is to get the group members to spend their time doing more important things – to spend MORE time in Q1 and Q2 and less time in Q3 and Q4.

So in a typical 40-hour work week (I know we all work more like 60 hours plus, I am talking about productive hours not busy hours doing nothing productive), the goal would be to spend 20 hours in Q1, 10 hours in Q2, 5 hours in Q3 and 2-3 hours in Q4. This helps prioritize the members' time in the most productive of ways.

I find that about 95% of the members of the mastermind groups strongly identify with the 1st triangle. As a group, we work on long term strategies, ideas, tasks and homework to understand how to switch that with better time management. We look at tracking your day and time…how you're REALLY spending you time. All the things that can help to move from Triangle 1 to Triangle 2.

Of course every member of the group struggles with different aspects of time management. And different members have strengths as well. That is where the members come together with insights and ideas that can help each other as well.

Q5 – Next we focus on How To Differentiate or Die By Becoming an Expert and an Authority In Your Field

Mastermind Groups

It's my philosophy that you need to differentiate your products or services you provide or you allow yourself to become a commodity, which means you will not survive in business for long. By becoming the expert and authority in your field, you can eliminate the doubt in people's mind as to IF they should use your products and / or services. By knowing you as an expert and authority they will have already decided that want you to solve their problem. The way we do this in the mastermind group is to work through several steps over the next couple of months as a group to help position themselves as experts first then to gain the authority. Those steps include:

a. Help Each Member To Write a Book – The business person needs to get their voice out in the marketplace and have their specialty stand out in the crowd. Some things we work through and encourage are:

i. Go to a book store or go online to Amazon and look at books and the chapter headings for their specialty. Find the chapter headings that look good and write them down. Gather them up as chapter headings you want to use in your own book.

ii. Go to forums and blog on the Internet in their field and find out what the hot topics are. What do people WANT to know about?

iii. These two things together become the basis for the content, headings and sub-indexes for the book.

iv. Decide if you want to write it yourself (takes time and time is money – can you take that time from your business?!?) or employ a ghost-writer. A ghost-writer can take the main topics, do much of the research needed and go to town. You still have the final say, you are still the expert, and it is still YOUR book.

v. Get the book self published.

vi. Once the book is published, work on ancillary products such and audio and DVD's.

b. Help members learn how to do lead generation.

c. Help members learn the ins and out of article marketing and press releases to build authority.

d. Discuss white paper and educational academic papers publishing and how it can help with authority and positioning.

The whole idea here is to make each member UNIQUE in their niche. To build each one of them as an expert and an authority in their field – not just "an expert" but "THE EXPERT & AUTHORITY". So when they go to an appointment or talk to someone on the phone, they have directed someone to a website, an article, a white paper, a book…something that has shown they are the expert and authority.

As an example, I'm able to do this myself. I pre-sell my services by sending a books and or audio products about myself to my potential coaching and consulting clients. I'm the expert and they know me before we talk in depth. I don't have to sell myself or my services. They already have the notion that they want me to help them out of the problem they are in and help them to grow their business. The final choice is with me the EXPERT & AUTHORITY to decide if I want to work with the client not the other way around, this is not to sound big headed but to emphasize who is in charge and who needs who.

So as we go back to the ideas above, my way of transforming businesses through my mastermind groups definitely incorporates long term strategies, accountability, changing the way of thinking, support and learning from the mistakes and successes of others. All of these things together help transform an ordinary business into an extraordinary business that will double or triple within three years.

TOBY: *Now it's time to take a good look at how the mastermind group changed and grew Toby's business. Remember, when we first met Toby, some of the specialized experiences he struggled with were:*

- *Business Planning*
- *Time Management*
- *Inventory Management*
- *Staff Management and Training*

Toby's group of local business owners had a wide variety of skills and experience. The style of his mastermind group was to let each person discuss an "issue" that they had in their business. The group would then ask questions and give input on that particular issue. Not everyone had an issue each week. That was fine with Toby…he had plenty to last for a while!

He felt one of his most pressing matters was staff management and training. With his brick and mortar shop getting reading to open up and the trouble he was having with his brothers in law, he really wanted to address this first. However, as members started digging in, they realized that he had never done a solid business plan. That was one of his first homework assignments. One of the members offered to mentor him outside of the mastermind group, which was extremely helpful. When he brought his business plan back, the members gave their input and Toby had a solid business plan for the first time in his 12 years of business!

With solid financial goals and milestones, his business looked completely different…it looked like a REAL business. He finally could see a plan for budgets, for training staff, for advertising, and what they could spend on marketing for their website. This gave Toby much more information to be able to come to the table with at the mastermind group sessions. And the personal development part was HUGE. It was a part he never even knew he was lacking. He felt like a business man instead of a surfer/college boy running a semi-business.

Instead of tackling staff next, Toby decided to tackle inventory management. The shop needed inventory ordered and this was not an area of expertise for him. Again, with the help of members, he was able to "Do as I say, not as I did" and learned some valuable lessons from other members who had brick and mortar stores. Of course their stores were different, but there was still valuable information to be gained.

When it came to staff management Toby brought it up in several of his mastermind group sessions. It was an ongoing issue. After six months he made some decisions. He had a sit down with both of his brothers-in-law individually. He let them know that he had made some major changes in his business, and they were going to need to make some major changes if they wanted to stay with him. He would give them one month to be on time every day, to be to every appointment on time and have all clients give a satisfactory rating. At that time, if all went well, he would promote them to territory manager. He had two territories he was going to split his route into. If they were made territory manager, he would hire them an assistant. If they were not promoted, they could work in the store for minimum wage, or they could find another job.

At the end of the month, one brother-in-law was promoted to territory manager and had completely changed his attitude. He was on time, professional and took the job seriously. As the mastermind group pointed out, sometimes what you convey is what you get! Toby taking himself more seriously helped his brother-in-law take himself more seriously as well.

The other brother-in-law had immediately asked to work in the store. He no longer wanted to be on the road, and wanted the opportunity to work in the store. He knew the tanks and equipment and offered to help Toby train staff in the store. Toby hadn't even thought of this, but it was a great solution! His brother-in-law WAS familiar with many of the systems and it worked out great.

Again, it was a matter of leading by example. Through the mastermind group, Toby had shown that he was open to new ideas and new ways of thinking. In the past, it had ONLY been he and his wife's way of thinking. Empowering his small staff was making a big impact on his business, and this was a direct result of the mastermind group way of thinking.

Time management was the other of Toby's problem areas. While is continues to be a constant battle with the level of activity in his life, he has gained a tremendous amount of insight from the mastermind group. He has learned from others the downfalls of spending too much time on business. One member had a heart attack at 42. He constantly lectures the other members on taking time to SLOW down and find a way to enjoy life. Toby has made sure to include a date night with his wife every other week. It's a start. No kids, and no work talk...just he and his wife.

So nine months later, Central Aquariums has opened and been open for 2 months. His brother-in-law is running the store efficiently and has done a great job training the staff. Toby does weekly training with the staff to make sure they are up to date. Toby's wife is running the website and marketing campaigns with ideas that have been generated from the mastermind group.

One of Toby's biggest worries was opening the store without losing his current clientele. His brother-in-law and other territory manager have kept the current clientele very happy. In addition, the mastermind group has had the added benefit of bringing in additional clientele to his customer aquarium and servicing base. The business plan that Toby put together allowed him to see where money was being poorly spent and allowed him to reallocate it.

He now spends his time acquiring new clients for the custom aquariums, does installation of the complex aquariums, and spends much of his time on becoming the local expert on all things aquarium-related (as suggested by his mastermind group). He goes to local schools to teach them about fish and coral reefs and is able to send home flyers in the kids' backpacks. He also holds classes at the store to teach people how to take care of a fish tank at no charge. This has brought in a significant amount of business.

Toby's retail business is going great, and his custom and service business has grown by 30%. He considers his mastermind group to be the driving force to growing his business.

ANDREA: Let's look at Andrea and how she has done with her start-up business and how her mastermind group has helped her. When we first met Andrea, the specialized knowledge that she struggled with was:

- Sales techniques
- Money management
- Marketing

Andrea was very excited about joining a mastermind group, and thought that the group would be of particular help to her in the following areas:

- Accountability
- Personal Growth
- Encouragement

- *Energy*
- *Synergy*

Andrea is seven months into her business and her mastermind group. As we know, she decided to turn the group over to a professional coach, but is still helping to run the group on an administrative level. The group has had a bit of a bumpy start, but the last four months or so have been pretty stable and the group is really gaining ground and making significant progress.

The group runs by having a "topic of the week" that is decided the previous week. Since all the members are internet marketers, most subjects have applied to most everyone. There have been very few complaints, with the exception of the odd "I don't need help with goal setting" complaint. (and really, who is perfect at that?!?).

Being internet marketers, marketing in various aspects has been a theme that has come up again and again. Although Andrea THOUGHT she had a good handle on marketing, she really had no idea how much more there was out there and available. She has gotten ideas on social media marketing, mobile marketing and Pay Per Click advertising that weren't part of her initial plan.

Not only have the ideas been presented, but she has learned the successes and failure of some of the other members of the mastermind group and has been able to "fast forward" her business decisions. She now has a Facebook Fan page, a LinkedIn profile and a solid Twitter following for her Autism site. She has also developed weekly podcasts and set herself as an expert in her field. Her eBooks and eCourses are available for sale on her site and are doing well.

With the help of her mastermind group she has really gotten over her fear of being a "salesperson". She has changed her mindset to being that "expert in her field" who has excellent products and services to offer. That mindset has made all the difference in her "sales techniques". When she is writing a "sales letter", she keeps that in mind. She is an expert in her field offering excellent products and services to clients who have a need.

She has also learned a tremendous amount about money management from her mastermind group. Again, from a "learn from my mistakes" point of view. It was refreshing to hear that others had trouble mixing personal with business monies in the beginning, but several people had GREAT ideas on how to separate the two. Andrea now feels much more empowered as she has met her "homework goals" to become more financially smart.

So let's see if the mastermind group met some of Andrea's other expectations and helped her to grow her business in other ways as well.

From an accountability perspective, Andrea feels like there is no way she would be where she is in her business without the mastermind group. The homework kept her focused and made sure she was making progress before each new session. She made sure her goals and action steps were done, and it helped her business tremendously.

While she still has insecurities, Andrea's personal growth has shot through the roof. Just STARTING the mastermind group was a big step for her. In the beginning, she was a little nervous to speak up and give her insights and opinions. Now, she is one of the first ones that will speak up. While she knows she has received plenty, she feels like she has given to, and that feels great.

The encouragement portion has been a lifesaver for Andrea. It seems like every time she hit a roadblock, a mastermind session was right around the corner, and encouragement would come in bucket loads. It also gave her the energy to just keep going. A mastermind group session where she learned something new would give her enough energy for days…or a week. Even if she was a little down, she would review her notes or listen back over the call and think of all the GOOD things that had happened to someone else on the call or something new she learned that she would eventually be able to implement in to her business. She knew growth for her business would come. If the others in the group could be successful, she knew that she could be, too.

And the synergy was just amazing. It was great to see the ideas that would form. Not just for Andrea's business, but for other's as well. Oftentimes an idea would start with ONE person's issue, but would end up being the solution for someone else. Synergy is a wonderful thing!

So seven months into her business, where IS Andrea? Well, she couldn't be happier. She has a solid following and name recognition in the autism community. Her blog is visited and commented on daily. And best of all, her info products are selling very well. She is doing well over £8,000 a month and is looking to add some physical products to the site as well. At the suggestion of the mastermind group, she is also considering a membership site.

Andrea loves her mastermind group. She is considering joining a second group…one that is geared towards an ever higher level of success. She will stay with her original group, but feels a second group may offer her even more.

Take a moment to think very carefully about your business.

Think about the beginning of the book and the things that you wanted to change or do better.

If you were nine months down the road, how would you want YOUR business to look?

What would be different?

How do you think a mastermind group could impact and grow your business?

Your Notes:

"Failure is simply the opportunity to begin again, this time more intelligently"

- Henry Ford

Chapter 17 - Turning an Average Business Into a

Success Story with a Mastermind Group

"Knowing is not enough, we must apply. Willing is not enough, we must do."

-Johann von Goethe

So let's take a look at the idea of what a mastermind group can do to a business a little more in depth. Let's take nine businesses and see how joining a mastermind group changed an average business into a success story.

Case Study #1 – An eBay Business

About 2 years ago, I was giving a seminar in London. During the lunch hour a gentleman that I'll call George came up to me and asked if a mastermind group could really help his business and deliver the results that I was talking about in the seminar.

George went on to explain to me that he ran an eBay store that sold low-value electronic items. His average price per item was about £39. George's company seemed to be doing quite well when you looked at it on paper. His turn over volume just on eBay was £1.2 million a year. He was operating on a profit margin of 30%. Yet he couldn't understand WHY for the past two years he was just barely scraping by. His business had broken the million mark, yet they were still just barely managing to make ends meet. They were juggling money and figures. They were robbing Peter to pay Paul in order to pay suppliers and their eBay listing fees. Something just wasn't right!! He really wanted to know if a mastermind group might help him to see something he was obviously missing.

Before deciding to join a mastermind mind group, George asked me if I would be willing to visit his business. Two weeks later I travelled up north to meet with George. George was very pleased to see me. He introduced me to all his staff members. He had been telling his staff about the seminar and about the potential of joining a mastermind group in order to help their business get a move on to help the business and the bottom line. After getting a tour, we began to knuckle down to some hard work. We started getting numbers and figures for the big picture.

George ran an eBay store with a turnover of £1.2 million that was started 3 years ago. George sells on average about 2,770 items a month that average £39 each. These are small electrical items ranging from small cameras, cordless phones, cigarette lighters, etc.

He had a total range of 5,000 lines depending on the season. George went on to explain that for every 100 items listed they would sell about 20 items. Therefore 80 items would not sell, but they would still have to pay the listing items for the other 80, and they would be relisted the next time around. They worked on profit margins of 30%.

At any given time they had about 10,000 items listed. Some were duplicates. Most of the information George had at hand. What he didn't have, he could get quickly.

What George could not understand was that he was bringing in over one million, yet he was struggling with cash flow and profits. WHAT was he doing wrong? He was putting in 10-15 hours a day, six days a week. Yet at the end of the day, he could probably go get a job and earn more money. George asked: "Do you think the mastermind group can help me and my business or should I just call it a day and walk away??"

I said, "Don't be silly?!?! You have a good business here!! You have hidden assets far greater than you realize." I suggested that

George join a particular mastermind group that I had in mind. I knew without a doubt that the people in that group would have some great insight for George and his business. What I told George is, "You have a beautiful viable business. You haven't even started to tap into your resources. Do NOT be disheartened!! You business can be increased substantially!!"

A week later, George joined us at our mastermind group. We had a group of 10 business men and women with varying types of businesses. Some were online and some were brick and mortar, yet all had some level of success. The group was a very cohesive one and had agreed that with George being the newest member, they would devote the session to him.

George laid out much of what he had told me. His biggest frustration being that he had hit the million mark, yet was still struggling to pay bills. At this point, George agreed to be put on "the hot seat". The other members of the group were allowed to ask him questions to which he answered. They then went around a second time to drill down deeper to ask some clarifying questions based on what some of the other members in the group had asked.

At this point, some suggestions and insights were given by the members of the group. And boy, were the insights eye-opening! The first one was that George's real assets in the business were the 60K strong customer base that he had built up over the past three years. He had customer first names, last names, addresses, and email addresses (which were the most valuable part). He was sitting on a gold mine! Like most people he treated this list with indifference. He allowed people to come in through the front door in eBay and leave by the back door. I am a great believer that once you acquire a customer you should build a relationship with that customer.

What the mastermind group pointed out was that George was so busy trying to acquire new customers on eBay and competing with other suppliers on price, etc, that he was leaving the real nuggets on the table. If a customer buys from you once and he is satisfied…there is a high probability that he will buy from you again and again and again. The highest cost for a company is to acquire a new customer. Once the customer has been acquired…the next time you sell to them, you don't have the marketing cost to sell to them again.

You could see the light bulb go **ON** in George's head. He understood. And yes, he felt a little dumb that he hadn't realized this on his own. But you see, that is what a mastermind group is all about. It's asking questions…asking more questions…and giving insight you may not have thought of before. Sometimes you get so busy doing the same things the same ways…you just can't think of another way of looking at your business. It's not uncommon.

That first session, George's head was reeling. He left with a goal: to think of how he could harness those current customers and sell to them again. When he came back the following month, his plan was to develop a newsletter to send out to his customer base on a weekly basis. A good idea, but he wanted to make it even better.

The mastermind group put their heads together and came up with some great ideas. George ended up running best buy deals for his customer base on a weekly basis over a three- month period. The special offers were generated JUST for his current customer base. George didn't even have to specially acquire these "specials". He didn't even own these items. They were subject to order, and he didn't have to worry about inventory orders. The idea was to give customers a VALUE of 20 – 50% off anyone else.

George ran trials of one month and realized that the response rate was MUCH greater than what he expected. In fact, it was so great, he sold more than he had available. He had to limit the number of special buys available with each news letter and best buys.

While the eBay store continued to bring in new customers, George focused on having existing customers buying MORE. Twelve months later, George's turnover went to £5.4 million. That's an over 4 million increase…WITHOUT having to increase inventory!

George's next goal is the 10 million stage to move to next level. He won't be leaving the mastermind group anytime soon! He continues to get solid advice on a regular basis. At the same time, George gives GREAT advice to members in the group as well. While George's business was above average in terms of the money he was generating, it was average in the terms of barely being able to pay the bills. With the help of a mastermind group, George's business is now a true success story!

Case Study #2 – Kahn's Restaurants

Several years back I was referred a client from a firm of accountants, a Mr. Kahn who had 9 local restaurants in their chain. Each restaurant had a capacity of approximately 107 people. When Mr. Kahn came to me, the restaurants were not doing very well. On the weekends (when they should have been at the height of their business), they were not even achieving 30% capacity. Not even 30 people were in the restaurant.

The restaurants were losing between £10,000 and £15,000 a month and had been doing so for nearly a year. Mr. Kahn and his partners felt that they could no longer sustain those substantial losses. They either needed a solution to turn the restaurants around or they needed to close the businesses and walk away with minimum financial damages to themselves and their interests.

I suggested to Mr. Kahn that he join a mastermind group that I had of very successful business owners. These were businesses that were sustaining profits in excess of £50,000 a month. I explained that by joining the mastermind group he would not be getting a "quick fix". He would need to be patient, and listen and learn from the others in the group. If the ideas were sound, he would need to implement them, and then evaluate them.

Mr. Kahn and his partners were sceptical. They were looking for the quick fix. It took some convincing for them to understand that slow and steady would be a better option. That tapping into the minds and ideas of these fellow business owner could be far better than just coming up with a quick plan and then another. Mr. Kahn and his partners finally agreed to give it a try, and it was agreed that Mr. Kahn himself would attend the mastermind group sessions.

The following month Mr. Kahn attended his first session. In that session he was able to tell the other business owners of his current situation and frustration with lack of filling capacity and therefore loss of profits. Many of the questions asked of Mr. Kahn that session cantered around his current advertising campaigns. Mr. Kahn explained that his main course of advertising was running ads in the local papers and in the Yellow Pages.

By the end of the first session the group had come up with an idea. The members of the group agreed to go to a few of the restaurants before the next session. They wanted to experience the food and the service to give Mr. Kahn any additional insights. Now that was a GREAT idea and support from the group!

Over the next two weeks, all of the mastermind group members visited one of the Kahn restaurants. When they came to the following mastermind group session they reported back. They found the food and the service to be exceptional!! So the problem wasn't in the restaurants themselves, it was simply that people didn't know about them.

The group continued to ask Mr. Kahn more questions. They went around in a round- robin fashion and would ask a question, which Mr. Kahn would answer. Then they went around one more time to ask any other questions based on the first set that was asked and answered. Finally, they went around a third time offering suggestions and insights.

The first thing that was proposed was that Mr. Kahn stop the local advertising and Yellow Pages ads as soon as the contracts ran out. These were obviously not effective and they were draining resources that were already in short supply. Mr. Kahn agreed to implement this as soon as the contracts were up.

The next strategy that was devised by the group as a whole was a localized coupon campaign. The idea was to design some simple coupons that would be handed out to hairdressers/salons within a two mile vicinity of each restaurant. Each salon owner would receive four complimentary vouchers to come down to the Kahn's restaurant for a meal and drinks with a partner…free of charge. The understanding was that if they enjoyed the meal and the service, they would place a postcard sized brochure on each of the mirrors at the stations within the salon. They would be able to use the other three vouchers at their discretion. They could reward top producers in the salon, do contests for their customers, or whatever else they chose to do.

The mastermind group members had a very specific reason the narrowed down the coupon campaign to the hairdresser/salon niche. The average woman is at the hairdresser for at LEAST a half an hour...some much longer. The hairdresser and client are always looking for something to chat about. If the card is on the mirror, it gives the client a chance to ask, "Oh, that card there, what restaurant is that for? Have you been there?" And it gives the owner or hairdresser the opportunity to talk about the great food and service that they experienced and to hand out a coupon for the client to try it themselves.

You see, what the mastermind group told Mr. Kahn is that from their experience NOTHING beats word-of-mouth advertising. Grass roots marketing can have a HUGE effect when done correctly. The other business owners in the mastermind group had great success using these innovative grass roots marketing methods and Mr. Kahn decided that he should listen to those in the room with successful and profitable businesses and give it a try.

In addition to the hairdressers, the other niche for the grass roots marketing strategy that was decided on was convenience stores. Although the customers weren't there as long, there are MANY customers a day and most of them are repeat customers.

Again, the mastermind group members assured Mr. Kahn that this was NOT a quick fix, but they also felt that is was something that could and WOULD turn his business around. It took about six weeks for Mr. Kahn and his partners to implement the plan. They got the vouchers, coupons and brochures delivered to the hairdressers and convenience stores around each of the restaurants.

Remember, Kahn's Restaurants was LOSING £10,000 to £15,000 a month. They started seeing improvements in the first 3 months. Within seven months they were breaking even. This was tremendous progress. Many businesses wait two years to be able to get to a break-even point. Mr. Kahn and his partners were thrilled. After 18 months the restaurants were making such a fantastic profit that a buyer came in and offered a significant amount of money to purchase the chain. Mr. Kahn and his partners were delighted with the offer and turned a keen profit.

The mastermind group has some VERY outside of the box thinking. It was not something Mr. Kahn or his partners would have ever considered. However, they were open minded enough to realize that there was rich experience in the group, and they listened to the input and suggestions. They implemented the ideas quickly and were able to reap the rewards. Mr. Kahn has gone on to join other mastermind groups that have helped him to be successful in his business endeavours.

Case Study # 3 - Jim's Auto Service Centre

Jim was a member of a Mastermind group that consisted of 11 strong members. Jim owned an auto service centre that did motor vehicle testing. Jim's business was well established with 20 years in the business. He had a staff of nine mechanics and his wife did the accounts and bookkeeping on a part time basis.

While Jim was bringing in about £935,000 a year, he kept brining up the issue of wanting to increase sales and profit margins as a topic in the mastermind group. As ideas were bantered around, Jim was still really frustrated and felt like he wanted to dig in deeper.

This particular Mastermind group decided to change directions at one point and do a complete in depth look at one business every few months in addition to covering a topic each time they met. Jim was the first to volunteer to have his business "overhauled"

Background: Jim gave this information as some additional background. He really felt as though the competition around him was starting to dig in and he was feeling the pressure.

The standard price for a MOT (road worthiness certification) for 12 months was £55 and it took about 30 to 45 minutes to complete. The competition was starting to offer the same certification at £25 to £35.

Jim simply couldn't afford to come down to those price levels. He had tried once or twice for "specials", but he couldn't maintain them long term.

Jim also used to be at a 150% margin on his peak days. His average sales were £180 to £200. He had about £140 in profit. Now he was servicing for £100 and clearing about £50. And sometimes, he was even taking a loss. Jim needed help.

The Mastermind group digs in: With ten other people in the group, it wasn't hard to have the group each make a visit to Jim's garage in between meetings. Each member agreed to stop by the workshop shop (not letting the staff know who they were), make some observations, ask some questions, and come back to compare notes the following session. Jim was also to bring printout of his financial books and customer records.

Each of the members of the Mastermind group had their own strengths and would be looking for certain things as they visited the shop and looks at Jim's printouts.

Observations: When the group came together the next time, it was amazing how similar the comments were! Most people had expected Jim's Garage to be a rather backstreet filthy kind of garage. It wasn't anything of the sort. His standards were WAY above the bar in terms of looks and cleanliness.

The problem was that Jim wasn't capitalizing on this. In fact, he was doing just the opposite, he had become a commodity.

What I mean by that is people didn't care about Jim's place because quite often they never even got that far. They would call up and ask for the price instead of ask what the service was like. The question was "How much do you charge?" then "Can you book me?" Jim was just a commodity. Anybody else can take your place when you a commodity.

He wasn't trying to educate the public or corporate sector about his services. When people don't understand about a product or service, the first thing they will do is ask you about price. However...when you educate your customers or clients to understand what it is you provide and what the benefits are, price doesn't have to be the main objective. It is a secondary or third or fourth issue down the line. Remember early on I mentioned about being the expert and authority?. That's how you move away from being a commodity that anyone can supply or being the expert that everyone wants.

So the group agreed that Jim's Garage was special, they just needed to come up with ideas that would help Jim to capitalize on what set him apart or COULD set him apart from the competition so he could stop being a commodity.

Customer Hot Points:

The group started by brainstorming some customer hot points that they or Jim thought could make a difference. Here are some of the hot points they came up with.

- I don't trust mechanics
- I don't understand anything under the hood of my car
- I don't want to get ripped off
- How do I know the mechanic knows what they are doing?
- I don't like to feel like I'm dumb
- Corporate – We already use someone else
- Corporate – Why would we switch?

Implementing Change

After further brainstorming within the group – there were some GREAT ideas that were given and then layered on and polished. Here are the final changes to his business that Jim decided to implement:

- Posters were made of bullet points highlighted the checkpoints for the procedures the Jim's Auto provided. These were in the workshop on the walls. These were to be pinpointed and shown to customers. This was taking pride in the workshop:

- A glass panel was installed in the customer reception area. When they came in, the customer handed the keys to the reception counter and filled out the paperwork. Then the customer would get a hardhat. Next they would be given a tour of the workshop. They would be shown that Paul handles Ford, Jim handles Honda, Simon handles Mitsubishi, and he'll be taking care of your car. It was a way of introducing the friendly staff and showing the service workshop. Then it was back to the reception area to let the customer sit down. If anything needed to be highlighted or brought to the customer's attention, the mechanic would get a hardhat and bring the customer to the car. There they would show them the physical problem on the car. If nothing was wrong, they would still bring the customer back and compliment them on what great condition the car was in.

- This is all bonding between the staff and customer. It helps alleviate the feeling of being ripped off and it builds trust. It also helps the customer not to feel "dumb", they are being educated at the same time. They are learning something.

- Before the car was let go, three helium balloons were blown up and put in the back of the car that say "Jim's Garage".

- For the corporate accounts, Jim sent out letters to his customers for the best testimonial. He would give the best testimonial an inclusive weekend for two to Paris…all expenses paid. He had never gotten better testimonials EVER!! People were writing one to two PAGES instead of paragraphs! He couldn't BUY testimonials like these for any amount of money.

- Corporate cars need to stay ON the road, not have any problems. These testimonials worked like a charm. Jim put all the testimonial letters in to a large binder and went out to potential clients and would run through his binder of testimonials with them. Jim emphasized service and safety more than price.

RESULTS

- Jim managed to sign 23 corporate accounts in two months.
- Customers kept coming back in and recommending more people.
- Referrals kept increasing
- Profit margin increased by 125% in six months
- Revenue is continuing to grow
- Jim no longer thinking inside the box!

•────────────────────────────────────•

Case Study # 4 - Paul's Auto Showrooms

Paul was a member of a London Mastermind class and had a problem. He had four used motor car showrooms scattered around the outskirts of London. He needed to turn his business around because he was either losing money or was breaking even at each one of his showrooms. Paul felt like he needed to do something drastic to make a change in his business.

I had seen the "focus group" work well on other groups, and encouraged this group to try it as well. They agreed to focus on Paul's showrooms as one of their first mastermind focus groups.

Background: The group started by putting Paul on the "hot seat" and asking him questions about his business. We took diligent notes and came up with items that we felt were of most importance to Paul and his business:

1) Paul was not doing any proactive activities.
2) Paul's main advertising budget was spent on ads in the local paper.
3) In all of Paul's showroom areas, the areas were quite well known for motor dealers. He had competitors on both sides at each of the four locations.
4) He advertising was a waste of time and money. The ads were bringing people to the AREA, but they would not necessarily

buy from HIM. In at least fifty percent of the cases the people would come in, look and then end up buying from someone else. This was advertising for someone else! Not wise at all.

5) Paul considered "everyone" to be his customer. In other words, he sold every variety of used motor car. All different makes and all different prices. He wanted to appeal to EVERYONE.

Suggestions from the group:

The group's feeling is that when you try to appeal to EVERYONE, you appeal to NO ONE. You simply can't have everyone as your customer and cater to them. The group strongly felt that Paul should consider narrowing down his niche. By having a VERY narrow niche, he would be different from his competition. He would learn to work with ONE manufacturer and become the expert or specialist for his customer base.

Paul agreed, and the process began to choose the manufacturer.

After some discussion without the group about pros and cons of different types of cars and their customer base, Paul decided on Land Rover as the manufacturer. Then the group decided to narrow down the niche even more. There are many types of Land Rovers.

The higher end Land Rovers are generally sold to construction firms or farmers. They are cash rich and don't buy second hand. So that is not a good model to go after.

The Discovery is often bought as a 2nd vehicle for wives. But again, these are usually for higher class families that go direct to the dealer.

However, many middle class families buy the Freelanders. And many of those will buy them second hand. So Paul decided on the Freelander. Then he narrowed down the niche even MORE by deciding to go with the diesel. They get better mileage and with the economy it is, should sell better. And then he narrowed the niche down one more time by deciding to go with Freelanders that were between a few months old to 3 years old.

Now, he could have gone even further with certain colours or options...but that is a pretty good narrowing of the niche! The group agreed that this was a narrow enough niche to specialize, but not too narrow to make it difficult to find and stock the showrooms.

The process:

After deciding to make the changes, Paul had some more work ahead of him. With the help of the group, he identified that he would need to:

- Change all signage and marketing materials
- Educate the sales staff extensively on Land Rover
- Educate the service staff extensively on Land Rover
- Make sure all advertising had the feel of SPECIALITY
- Start building a database of Land Rover owners

Results:

Within three months, all four of the showrooms had 15 Freelanders each that met the specifications ready to go.

It took six months to get the staff trained and ready and the materials switched over.

Paul found that with the "specialist" feel, he could charge upwards of 10% more for his vehicles without having to offer a discount because people felt reassured and comforted going to Paul's showrooms. They knew they would get a used vehicle from a Land Rover specialist and would be able to bring it back to be serviced to someone who knew how to work on the vehicle. They would go to him over the competition, even at a higher price.

As Paul started building his database of people who owned Freelanders, he was able to start selling service agreements and other products. He was able to build his database up to 10,000 people!

Paul even began to offer specialty products. He had Land Rover floor mats specially made in China that cost him under £20 each with shipping and everything else included. Most floor mats sold for around £150. Paul sent out a newsletter to his database and offered the floor mats at £49.99 plus postage, but let the customers know he only had 2,000. He sold out immediately!

Now once a month Paul brings in some sort of specialty line that he can offer to his clients at the time he sends out his newsletter. He has had great success.

The moral of Paul's story is that you must specialize in SOMETHING – you can't be everything to everybody! The group helped Paul to see the light, and it definitely led to his success.

Case Study #5 - Catering Business

One of the most common things I come across…without a doubt… is hearing a client say, "If I had more money I could do…."

Or

"If I had more money I could grow my business"

Or

"If the bank would only give me more money, I would FINALLY be able to….."

It never ceases to amaze me how many people think that more money will solve all their business problems. The fact of the matter is bad management - no matter WHAT – will swallow that money up. And if you get more, the same thing will happen.

Nine times out of ten, it's really an old mindset that gets in people's way. It's an old traditional way of thinking. It's looking at what everyone else is doing as opposed to thinking outside of the box. In all my mastermind groups I help them to expand their minds and way of thinking.

That's what a Mastermind group does for people most of the time. It just SHAKES them out of the traditional way of thinking. It gets them to STOP looking at what everyone else in their niche or business model is doing and encourages them to open their mind to different ways of thinking.

And once the mind is open, wonderful thinks happen. Once a mind is opened, it can be very hard to close! It just keeps thinking of new and innovative ways of doing things!

For this case study, I'd like to share with you the story of a student who was in a Mastermind group of nine other business owners. The student owned a catering business that was doing well. He wanted to expand in to another city.

The student went to the bank for a loan of £200,000 to start a kitchen in the new city. The bank said no, they were not prepared to loan them any more money. The climate was bad and £200,000 was simply too much money. Besides, while their business was doing well, it only making marginal money. Not enough for the confidence of the bank to provide such a large sum.

When the student came to the Mastermind group the session after getting the word back from bank, he was very discouraged. He wanted to get the groups ideas, but in a very specific way.

His questions went along these lines:

1) Does anyone know of any private investors?
2) Does anyone know of someone who would loan the £200,000 against shares?
3) Does anyone know of someone who would do part loan and part equity?

You see, he was thinking along ONE way, and one way only. I need £200,000 to open up a second catering business in a new city. That is the only way I can do. I can't get the money from the bank, so how else can I raise the money. In his mind, he WAS being somewhat open minded. He wasn't looking for another traditional bank!

As the moderator of the group, I did ask a couple of key questions to get the group trying to think in some new directions. The first question I asked was:

What would the £200,000 buy you?

I wanted him to think (and tell the group) how far £200,000 would really go. He proceeded to tell us that it would go towards buying the premises, and then making sure that changes were made to meet the health and safety standards. If any money was left over, it would go towards buying equipments.

So the £200,000 really wouldn't go that far. It was just to get a kitchen location, and get it ready to be able to meet health and safety requirements in order to cook food in.

Next I asked some other questions:

How much would you use the kitchen in the beginning as you are starting out?

How many hours per day? How much staff would it take?

How would that change in 3 months? Six months? One year? Two years?

Now the student started talking about his growth plan. Or rather lack of one! The group together came up with some great ideas on growth strategies. But that was a side note.

The fact of the matter was the student THOUGHT he was dead in the water. With no money, he didn't think he would be able to open a second kitchen.

I asked the group to do something for me…and especially for the student. I asked them to help the catering owner see that you should never limit their mindset on thinking in the traditional way. I wanted them to REALLY brainstorm on other ways that the catering owner to grow his business taking in to account the things that we had learned in the session.

It was a fantastic brainstorming session. It was Mastermind group thinking at its best with idea after idea forming. The catering owner was starting to get more energized as the ideas kept flowing.

The final idea that came from the session that night was this. The catering owner was to go to Manchester (the area that he wanted to grow) and visit 20-30 pubs. The economy was not doing well and most pubs were not running to full capacity. His goal was to go to the larger pubs and find a pub that had the facility that he needed, but wasn't being used to full capacity. He was to then work out an arrangement with the pub owner to have the facility loaned out to him for a fee when it wasn't in use.

The benefit was twofold. It would help the pub owner by bringing in extra cash. And it would help the caterer by not having to outlay a large amount of money. The facility is already in place AND it already meets the health and safety standards. And it probably has much of the needed equipment as well.

The other benefit to the catering owner is that is it less of a risk. He could try a new area and if it doesn't work out for some reason, he isn't sitting on a £200,000 loan. He has much less risk to his pockets and liability.

By the time the catering owner came back to next session he had seen a number of pubs. He stuck a deal with one of the pub owners. The deal ended up working out FANTASTIC. It was good for the pub owner and good for the catering owner. A good joint venture thanks to the collective thinking of the Mastermind group.

Case Study #6 – Financial Broker

Our next case study is another case of avoiding doing what everyone else is doing. I had a financial broker in one of my Mastermind classes for six months who was still having trouble growing his business. It's business with a LOT of competition. And unfortunately, most everyone does the same thing as everyone else.

Earl Nightingale said: "If you want to succeed, have someone to lead, coach or mentor you. If you can't find someone – look and see what everyone else is doing and do the total opposite"

It's true. Most everyone will fail in business. You HAVE to do something different if you want to be one of 5% or 10% that survive. Being in a Mastermind group is certainly a first step. Not everyone does that!

Back to our financial broker. Just like EVERY OTHER financial broker, he was running ads in the Yellow Pages, newspapers and online. It's what he was taught by his "boss" to do. But it was costly for any lead he did acquire. He had to pay for his Ad Sense, ads, whatever, and it just didn't make up for the leads he got. There just wasn't enough business out there. He was really getting frustrated.

One of the great things about a Mastermind group is that you can learn about what works in other sectors from people who have actually had success. Try to adopt something from another sector and see how it can apply to your business.

In a session of total frustration, the financial broker offered to go on the hot seat. He said he didn't care if he was "beaten up"! He wanted as many questions fired at him as possible...he would answer any and all questions. And he looked forward to going over any suggestions.

As the questions were going around round robin, many of them focused on what he was doing currently. Of course the answers were Ad Sense, Yellow Pages, and newspaper ads. As the group asked about his return on investment, he said it was little to none.

Then I thought let's throw the group a bone and see what they can make of it? interesting question that changed the focus of the evening. The question I threw in was "How do you work on getting repeat customers?"

The financial broker's answer was, "We don't have repeat customers".

The next question was, "Can you explain why you don't have repeat customers?"

The financial broker's answer was: "Well, I am in a business that once you acquire someone, it's very unlikely that someone will get ANOTHER mortgage in the next 5 to 10 years. I mean it happens, but not very much in this climate especially. Refinancing every few years is a thing of the past".

Things went in to full swing Mastermind mode after that!

The next question was: "If I'm a landlord, is there a possibility that I buy multiple properties?"

The financial broker's answer was: "....yes...."

The next question: "Could a landlord or property owner be a repeat customer?"

The financial broker's answer was and eye opening "YES!"

After the round robin, the group broke in to more of a brainstorming session to talk about the possibilities of landlord/multiples property owners. The guess was that most probably add to their portfolio on a regular basis.

The group identified a "prospect" as any landlord that has two to three properties. The financial broker was to look in local papers, on streets, etc to find prospect landlords that had two to three properties.

Next, he was to do whatever it took to take that person on! Be the BEST in personal service. He decided to have literature made up that talked about how he specialized in the multiple property owners and understood their special needs. He made sure to meet them where it was convenient for THEM as a busy business person instead of always suggesting they come to his office. Everything was catered towards the property owner and keeping them happy.

The financial broker was very excited to take on this new line of business. He decided to start with multiple property owners within a 20 mile radius, and then expanded to 30 miles and then to 50 miles. Within 12 months he had 45 landlords with multiple sales.

So, financial brokers CAN have repeat customers. And there IS other ways of looking at things. You just have to have an open mind.

Case Study # 7 - Solar Power Panels

This particular case study is a newer member of one of our Mastermind groups. Sometimes we will have members that will be in the group for months or even a year and make slow, but steady progress. Other times, a new member will jump in "guns blazing" and want to make a significant change right off the bat. Such is the case with this particular client.

This client is a distributor of solar power panels that are imported from Dubai to the U.K. Our mastermind student out of the top100 in solar panel distributors in the UK is about number 85, which is in the bottom list of players.

When the student came in to the Mastermind group the first night, they announced that their goal was to be in the top 20 distributors within 12 months. That was why they joined the mastermind group, and that they hoped to get ideas and suggestions that would help propel them to the top. THAT would make the Mastermind group a success in their mind.

No pressure!

This particular group is made up of a variety of successful business owners across various business sectors. They are always up for a challenge, and they had no problem diving in and asking our new member some tough questions. Here were some of the top questions:

- Do you install and distribute, or just distribute the solar panels?
- How do you advertise?
- How long do you keep on installer once you get them?
- How much does it cost you to acquire a client?
- What is your quality compared to competitors?
- How do you convey your quality?
- How do you find your installers?

All VERY good questions. You see, that is part of the strength of a mastermind group. They can help you to think of questions that you wouldn't even THINK of asking yourself. Sometimes it's a "How could I have never thought of that?!?!?" type of question. The answer is you are simply too close to the situation.

Having someone that is a step away can bring a different perspective to the situation. They can ask you an insightful question that can get you thinking in a completely different direction. It can open your eyes to new possibilities.

Such was the case with our new member. There were several questions that he couldn't answer right off the bat. Some of those included how much it cost to acquire a client and how he found his installers.

By the next few sessions, he was able to answer all of the questions. Here were his answers:

- He had no interest in installing the solar panels. He only wanted to provide the panels as a distributor to installers.
- He currently advertised through trade magazine ads and online
- After careful consideration and studying his advertising costs, he realized that is cost him between £2,000 and £3,000 to acquire each client.
- If he was able to look after them well, he could keep an installer for five to seven years.
- His quality was above average compared to his competitors. His closest competitor was a more well known brand, who also makes Pens. However, his quality was better. His prices did not reflect the better quality.
- He did not convey the higher quality in any literature or in prices. Nothing conveyed the high quality in any way.
- He currently found his installers through trade magazines or in other ads.

Group Suggestions:

Of course the fun comes as the brainstorming begins. This is a pretty high level, high thinking group, and the ideas flow freely. Here are the ideas that were given that the client agreed to try:

1. Finding new installers. One person in the group new of a site that the government runs to find various workers for working on houses. People can find a list of installers on the web. This is a fantastic readymade list for our client! It doesn't get much easier! The goal was to find a list of installers that did 2 or more installations per month and contact them.

2.   Convey the quality. The suggestion was made to up the price on the client's solar panels. He had a very fair price, and could afford the mark up without losing market place. With the mark up, he would also clearly convey the quality in all marketing materials. He had to show that he had VALUE that he was proud of.

3.   In order to KEEP the installers, he needed to make life as easy for them as possible. A fantastic idea was given by one of the members in the group that was expounded upon. It morphed in to this eventual idea. For every 10 installations that an installer did, the client would give them £10,000 towards advertising their service to the public. The caveat was that they had to bring the ad that showed that the ad featured the client's brand of solar panels instead of any other kind. That the installer exclusively used THEIR brand of solar panel. The installer got free advertising and the client got more exposure.

I admit that the client bemoaned this at first. He didn't understand why he should subsidize the installer when he was not making money at first. But you see, it's about creating a LONG TERM relationship and keeping their trust. There is a saying that goes, "people don't care how much you know until they know how much you care".

Our client soon learned that the installers were fiercely loyal to him. They could not believe they had found a distributor that believed and invested in their business. They would not use any other distributor. In six months time, the client has acquired many new installers and is well on his way to hitting his goal!

Case Study #8 – Residential Property Owner

Peter is a residential property owner that belongs to a mastermind group of eight local members. He has been in the group for about a year and a half. Peter has always been a very active and vocal part of our mastermind group. He has enjoyed a good business over the years and has always had valuable input to give to the other members in the group.

The financial downturn has affected MANY people's businesses, and it certainly has affected Peter's. As you can imagine, the economy has been tough on Peter as a residential property owner. Peter generally buys residential properties that have been run down or have been repossessed by the mortgage company or bank. Of course the idea is to get them at a good price.

Peter then puts the time and money in to refurbishing and repairing them with anything they need. He may modernize, remodel or redecorate as a particular property or house needs. After giving the house the refurbishing and repairs it needs, he turns around and sells it...hopefully at a healthy profit.

The biggest problem for Peter in the economic downturn is quite simply money. Peter can only afford to work and manage turning around one to two properties at a time. Ideally, he would like to be working on turning around five to six properties at once. However, he would need to have more people working for him. More importantly, he would need more capital.

You see, you have to BUY the property and the materials to fix up the properties. The bank will only loan so much money when they see that you already have an outstanding loan out. And when you buy the materials, you also have to pay the labourers to do the work on the property. It's a large outlay of cash per property before it can even be worked on...let alone sold and then work on reinvesting the money in to the next property.

Finally, it was Peter's turn to turn to the mastermind group for some help. A few months ago when the group had a lull, Peter sheepishly raised he hand. He said that he had wanted to ask the group for some advice for a while, but had been reluctant to do so.

You will sometimes see this happen with "the confident one" in the group. They are oftentimes the one that is quick to give advice...and they often have GREAT ideas...the rest of the group tells them so on a regular basis. They are looked at as an informal "leader" of the group because they often have such great ideas.

The drawback for the person can be that they feel "less" of a business person when they have an issue. Of course this is silly! EVERYONE has issues in their business. Everyone should always feel confident and comfortable bringing up all of their concerns. But while some people may share superficial concerns on a regular basis, it may take much longer before they share deeper concerns. Such was the case with Peter.

Peter stated to the group that REALLY wanted to get to the point that he could work on five to six properties at a time. He had been to several banks, and tried some private lending options, but because of the current economic conditions, it didn't look like he was going to be able to raise the capital he needed.

Peter was honest is saying that he felt like there was SOME OTHER option out there, but he was really stuck in this "I need more capital" mindset, and he just was having a hard time thinking outside of that box. He needed the help of the group to brainstorm and come up with some other ideas and options.

The group started throwing out some ideas…but the first round really seemed to centre around capital still. In the second round, the questions started to focus more on the PROCESS of what Peter did once he had the property. Here are some things that the group was able to find out:

1. While Peter had SOME key craftsmen/specialists that he liked to use, he oftentimes was looking for someone to hire. For instance, he may have a favourite plumber, but if that plumber wasn't available, he would have to god to number 2, 3 or 4 on his list. The same with electricians, painters, plasterers etc.
2. The issues with this was time was of the essence for Peter. Ideally, he wanted to turn a house around in ONE MONTH. If he spent part of that time hiring his crew, time was lost. And if it was a crew that was further down his list, chances were they either took longer or their quality wasn't as good.
3. Peter knew if he has a SOLID and LOYAL group of craftsmen/specialists, this could help him with his overall time frame.

The question became a little clearer to the group. Peter needed to:

1. Be able to increase his properties from one to two a month to five to six a month
2. Reduce his capital/overhead costs to be able to do that
3. Build up a sold and loyal group of craftsmen/specialists to speed up his turn around

The group felt that if Peter could work on goal numbers 2 and 3, if would help him to achieve goals number 1. The question was how to accomplish that. A terrific answer came from a member of the group that owned an electrical company. While he didn't do residential work, he brought up the idea of joint ventures.

His suggestion was this: If Peter were to joint venture with the craftsmen/specialists it could be a win/win for both sides. The craftsman/specialist would do the work at no cost as in investment. When the house was sold, they would receive part of the profits...profit sharing. Depending on the type of business, the craftsman or specialist may be willing to provide the materials at no upfront cost as well, in exchange for part of the profits.

The benefit to Peter would be in several areas. First, he would not have to outlay the cash for the materials or the labour. Second, if he could find the craftsmen/specialists who would be willing to do this, it would be a small pool that would build up loyalty if he treated them very fairly in the profit sharing. And lastly, since they were getting a part of the profits, it would be incentive for the craftsmen/specialist to work at an accelerated rate. At least this is what Peter and the group thought would happen!

Peter decided to give it a try. It took him between two and four months to find all the appropriate people. Some skills he was able to find sooner.

Peter was excited and nervous to see how the first project would go! He bought his first "JV house" and brought in his partners. The first JV house was turned around in four weeks! And at a nice profit! Mission accomplished.

Peter found a very unexpected side effect happened. As the continued success of the JV partnerships went on, the JV partners were making more money and wanted to chip in MORE money on the front end and get more on the back end. This worked out to Peter's advantage. He was able to rely less and less on the banks.

Peter was happy to give the JV partner's more of a share as they pitched in more on the front end. He didn't have to put as much money in, which meant that he was able to work on more houses at one time. He was able to meet his goal of five to six houses at a time, and then exceed it. The profit his was able to make was well worth what he was giving his JV partners.

Case Study # 9 – Property Maintenance Company

Steve is a member of a mastermind group from a suburban town. The group has 9 members that are very active and Steve has been in the group for about 2 years now. Steve has a property maintenance company that deals mostly with residential homes.

Steve has been an active member of the group, and has always been honest with how his business is doing. When he first joined the group, Steve's business was doing well, but he needed some help with getting the word out and needed some general business skills help as well. He has done very well improving his business and has also helped other members in the group.

The last six months have been hard on Steve. Business has been declining due to the highly competitive nature of the competition in this economic climate. As the larger companies have seen some major downsizes in their large accounts, they have gone after the "little guys" business and are undercutting them on price.

Steve runs a very good property maintenance company, but he can't afford to go toe to toe on price with the larger companies. He needs to grow his business, but he knows he needs to do it on something other than price alone. Everyone else in the market is price driven.

The group in general has seen what "price driven" does to companies. It's very against any "price drive only" campaign. That's not to say that price can't be a PART of a campaign, but it can't be what you hang your hat on. The group has brainstormed and seen some VERY GOOD results as they help each other come up with innovative ideas. Steve knows this and was looking very forward to what the group could do for him.

Even when you are in a mastermind mind group, you can still be a little bit stubborn at times! You understand the possibilities that the mastermind group can bring to you and your business…but you may be reluctant to bring up your issue to the group. You may feel like you "can" or "should be able to" handle whatever challenges come your way. This is common with business owners, and it's why so many business owners get stuck and keep themselves from moving forward. It's why many businesses fail. They don't seek help and they don't take opportunities that are right in front of them.

When you are in a mastermind group you always have to tell yourself that you are in the group, and you need to USE THE GROUP for what it is there for. You joined the group to help grow your business. If you don't use it for that purpose, it's really a shame! Your business deserves more!

Luckily Steve was able to realize that the group would be good for helping him think outside the "price driven" box.

As the group started to tackle Steve's property maintenance business, they looked at what Steve could do on the FRONT END that would help him long term on the BACK END. It was something this particular group looked at a lot as they stayed away from a price driven competitive market.

The strategy was often to find something the set a business apart on the front end. Something that would build up customer loyalty and long term clients. While the front end may have something that would be at a break even or even loss from a cost perspective, it would be well made up for in the long run (see case study #7 – the solar panels with the advertising paid for with 10 installations is another great example of this).

Of course it would need to be something that was a value or perceived value to customers…without completely breaking the bank as well.

The group went to work brainstorming on all kinds of ideas. They included weeding services, lawn mowing services, fence repair and more. It needed to be something that virtually everyone would want or need, especially if it were at a good enough price.

Steve and the group finally settled on the perfect front end service – window cleaning. Everyone loves to have nice clean windows, but it's a job that few people really like doing themselves. It's a job that gets pushed to the bottom of the list.

The going rate for window cleaning for the outside of a house was £15 to £20. It took about ½ hour to do the front and back of a house. Most houses like to have their windows cleaned about every two to four weeks.

The goal of Steve's front end was this:

1. Decide which housing developments he wanted to dominate
2. Hire 10 window cleaners
3. Set up the cleaners in teams of 2 (due to local laws)
4. Get nice uniforms for window cleaners with the name of Steve's property maintenance company clearly visible on them
5. Charge £10.00 per house for cleaning.

Now, you may say…I thought price driven was not the goal here?!? It's not. Because window cleaning is NOT THE GOAL here. Window cleaning is just the front end means. It was a way for Steve to get in the door and dominate an area.

The next part of the front end equation was this:

1. The window cleaners were to be the eyes and PR of the property maintenance company. They had to not just do a good job, they had to do 100% job and go over and above the normal requirements – they had to WOW the customers.
2. The window cleaners had to be trained to be vigilant. They had to look out for leaky drain pipes and overflowing gutters. They had to look for rotting doors and window. They had to keep an eye out for fences that needed repairs or anything else around the house that Steve's company could help with.

3. If they saw ANYTHING that needed to be repaired they either had to report it to Steve or give a brochure to the client and say, "oh, did you know we also do "....". If you like, I can have someone give you a call.

It took three months for the window cleaners to all have steady jobs in the housing developments that Steve wanted to dominate. In the beginning it cost Steve a little extra money. It didn't take long before he was breaking even.

The back end definitely paid off! After twelve months Steve had built up a VERY loyal customer base. His window cleaners were doing their job brilliantly on the front end, and his maintenance business had DOUBLED in size!!

All by a simple mind change!

"Formal education will make you a living; self-education will make you a fortune"

- Jim Rohn

Chapter 18- What To Do Next

"Before everything else, getting ready is the secret of success."

- Henry Ford

So now that you've learned all about mastermind groups, the question becomes what to do next. The following is a bit a review…as well as a help for your next steps. It's a checklist to help you move forward and make a difference in your business. So let's get started:

__ **What skills or knowledge do you need to improve in your business?**

Think about the skills and knowledge that you already have in your business. You probably already have things that you are very comfortable with and are working very well for you. Take a few minutes to think about what skills or knowledge you may not be as strong in. What skills or knowledge…if you were better at…do you think could improve your overall business?

- **Business**

- **Marketing**

- **Record keeping**

- **Money management**

- **Time management**

- Customer service
- Sales techniques
- Technical know-how
- Inventory
- Staff management and training

- What benefits of the mastermind group appeal to you?

Everyone has a different aspect of the mastermind mind group that appeals to them. It's important to identify when benefits appeal to you. You want to make sure are you go forward with your mastermind group that you look back occasionally and make sure that the mastermind group is meeting these needs.

- **Personal Growth**
- **Resources**
- **Differing Perspectives**
- **Mutual Support**.
- **Encouragement**
- **Energy Experience**
- **Specialized Knowledge**
- Synergy

- What type of mastermind group do you think would be a better fit for you?

You'll want to make sure that you join a mastermind group that fits your particular needs. The first fit that you'll want to take a look at is a vertical or horizontal mastermind group. As a quick refresher, a vertical group is when all members are a part of one niche or industry. A horizontal group includes members from a variety of industries.

- **Vertical**

- Horizontal

- Which method of mastermind group do you prefer?

The next part of the type of mastermind group is the location base. For some, the in- person if best (and is the preferred method if possible). For some, internet or phone based mastermind groups will be more practical.

- In-person mastermind group

- Internet or phone-based mastermind group

- Start your search for a current mastermind mind group

Now the fun begins! It's time to start looking for current mastermind groups that are running that you can join. Don't forget to ask about meeting times, guidelines, agendas, size of the group and anything else that is important to you.

- Ask friends/work colleagues

- Meetup.com

- Facebook

- LinkedIN

- mastermindcoach.com

- Chamber of Commerce

- Forum/Message Boards

- General Internet Search

- What looked promising?

- Do trial session for any groups that are possibilities

- What is important to you in a mastermind group?

As you do a trial session for any of the groups, make sure to pay attention to any of these things that are of particular importance to you.

- **Success of members**
- **Number of members**
- **Business type of members**
- **Location of members**
- **Proactive group (paid professional coach)**
- **Reactive group (group led coach)**
- **Rigid agenda**
- **Loose agenda**
- **Day/Time of meeting**
- **Other (list)**

- **Find a group that fits**

- **If no group, will you start a group?** How will you do this?

- **What do you want to achieve from joining a mastermind group?** Write a thoughtful answer.

- **How soon do you want to achieve it?** Set a specific date

While this list is not meant to be exhaustive, it's a good place for you to start to take the next step. I hope you have enjoyed learning about the mastermind groups. More importantly, I hope you will take the information and implement it in your business. I assure you that if you do, amazing things will happen!

Chapter 19 – FAQ's

There are sure to be plenty of questions that have come to your mind as you've been reading this book. I hear questions all the time as I work with clients and potential clients. I've compiled some of the most frequently asked questions I get here and answered them for you.

1. **I've heard two different things – one is that you should get other "like minded people" and other is that you should only join a group that has people who are doing "better than you currently are" so as to push yourself. Which one is right?**

    You may get tired of hearing this answer…but there is no "right or wrong". There most certainly are differing opinions. It's good to take a look at the differing opinions, and then make the final decision based on your situation and what feels best for YOU.

    Let me say this though – you should ALWAYS be looking for a group that has "like minded people" to some degree or another. That doesn't mean that they all think like you. It doesn't mean that they have the same business as you. They don't even have to have the same exact goal as you. But they should be working towards a same common goal. They should have an open mind about the power of the mastermind. They should be positive and excited about what the mastermind group can do for everyone in the group. Like minded is not a cookie cutter of each other. It's a commonality of some kind that is threaded throughout the people in the group.

As far as the second point goes – there are certainly a consensus of people that believe you should only join a group of people that are in a way "better" than you. But that gets to be impossible doesn't it? Not everyone can join a group of people who are already better than them…there would be no group to join! The general idea is that you want to stretch yourself, and that is a good thing. But everyone is at a different part of the life and their business. For some people, just dipping their toe in to the idea of joining a mastermind group is good enough for now! For others, YES….stretch yourself…join a group of people who are that "next level" up from where you are. Just make sure you are giving as much as you are getting!

It would be like saying I would like to play golf with Tiger Woods every weekend but where is the challenge for Tiger to play golf with you? Do you get my point? Good.

The point is, there is no perfect way to join a mastermind group. Joining a group is what is important. Do what feels right to you in your business at this time. You can always join a different or another mastermind group later!

2. What makes a good purpose for a mastermind group?

Again, there is no perfect answer to this question – except to say that the more defined and to the point the better. A broad purpose such as "to increase the sales of the members" does not give the group much of a purpose. What business doesn't want to increase its sales? How much of an increase would the group like to increase and by when?

If it's a group of internet marketers, is there a common goal of increased traffic, conversation rates or page rankings?

It could be something that is not totally business related. The group could have a common purpose of increasing their business to a level of being able to contribute £2,000 a month to a certain charity.

It doesn't matter WHAT the purpose is. As long as there is a defined and focused purpose, the mastermind group can be working towards that purpose. When there is a lull in conversation or perceived progress, the group can always go back to the purpose and say, "What have we been doing to move closer to our purpose as a group and individuals? How can we do it better?"

3. **When it comes to finding a mastermind group – are there really other like minded people out there?**

This is one question that comes up a lot! Especially because so few people are aware of the fact that mastermind groups even exist. So when they are enlightened, they wonder if there are other people out there who could possibly know about mastermind group and be interested in being a part of one.

While there are many people who DON'T know about the power and effectiveness of mastermind groups, there are many who do. Some have been in mastermind groups before and are looking for a new mastermind group to join. Some belong to a group already, but are interested in joining another one or two groups that have a different purpose. They REALLY understand the power of the mastermind group and realize that they can achieve different results from different mastermind groups.

What this question really comes down to is: are there other like-minded people who are open to the concept of the mastermind group? Let me rephrase it. Do you think there are other people out there who might be interested in learning from others? Who might be open to growing their business and their lives in a new way? Who might enjoy the power of a group of minds being more powerful than their single mind? The answer is definitely yes. There are plenty of other like minded people out there who are willing to be a part of a mastermind group.

4. **If I'm starting my own group, how do I find those people?**

Even though we talk about this in a specific chapter, this is STILL something that people really worry about. Are there people out there who might want to join and group and how in the world do I find them?

First, go back and re-read Chapter 11 – it tells you some great place to advertise for others to get the word out for a newly forming mastermind group.

As with almost anything, word of mouth is your best form of marketing and advertising. (Remember Mr. Kahn and his success story!). Talk to people who are in business and see if they know others who are interested in joining a mastermind group. You can "talk" in person, emails or on social media networks. The point is to get the word out.

When you are talking about the mastermind group that you're starting, let people know what KIND of person you're looking for. Talk about the qualities of who you are looking for. Not only does this let them know that you are looking for someone like them…it lets them know the mastermind group will consist of LIKEMINDED people…with these types of qualities. After all, these are the qualities you are seeking.

When you are excited and positive about starting a group, positive minded people will be attracted to you. You will probably find yourself with a full group in no time!

5. Is it hard to break down the barriers and really get to know and trust each other in a group? Especially when it comes to detailing out important business principles?

The trust issue. It comes up over and over again. Sometimes I'm not sure if people are asking if others will be able to trust, or if they are really asking if THEY will be able to break down the barriers and trust!

Let me just say it doesn't happen immediately. The first couple of sessions are definitely about getting to know each other. Sure, you may have one or two people who are just naturally "open book" types of people and don't mind laying everything out on the table from the get go. But that is unusual. Most people are a little more reticent in the beginning, and it takes some time to get to know each other and build upon the trust before things open up.

One thing that people will often ask is "how can I make sure that some great idea I talk about isn't going to be stolen". Well, you probably won't talk about your great idea on the first session. You'll know when the time is right and when you feel like you trust your group and you can give details on a project or idea that you have. Before that, you can give more generalizations.

I've honestly not seen a mastermind group where people are out taking ideas they heard and turning them in to their own. Most people are just too busy working their own business! Yes, your idea is important to YOU, but you need to realize that other people have different ideas and businesses that are important to THEM! They don't want your idea, they want to better their own business.

So when it comes to trust, the best advice is to take a deep breath and….go with your gut. When you are ready to talk about a certain level of your business, go for it. If someone asks you a pointed question, and you're not ready to go in to that much detail, just say, "I'm not at that comfort level yet! Hopefully in another few sessions I'll be there!". That kind of honesty is what will bring the trust level up and break down the barriers in the group.

Remember you don't HAVE to share anything you don't want to when it comes to specific business details. You don't have to share numbers or names. Just what you are comfortable sharing that would be valuable information to help another member in the group. It's the EXPERIENCE and what you learned from it that tends to be the most value.

In the end, time takes care of breaking down the barriers. It often happens much quicker than you would imagine!

6. **I'm a really busy person, and I just don't know if I can commit to showing up each meeting. Should I still consider joining a mastermind group?**

If you really think you can't commit to a mastermind group on a regular basis, I would seriously reconsider joining. It's simply not fair to the other members.

Here's what typically happens when members show up sporadically. The first part of the meeting is spent go over some of the goals from last time, and the people who weren't there inevitably have a question or input on what was previously discussed. Then as the meeting progresses and someone refers back to something that was discussed last session, someone who wasn't there will ask for it to be explained. Time is spent going back over the item. Often times the person who wasn't there will have input or insight, and the item is REHASHED. This is re-hashing instead of moving forward.

Progress is often slow in a group that has members that are frequently missing. Of course circumstances do come up that you can't help and sometimes you will miss a meeting. However, if you know it's going to be regular, evaluate if this is really a good step for you right now.

That being said, I would like to make another observation. I have had plenty of people join a mastermind group thinking they were "busy people". One of the eye opening parts of the mastermind group was finding out that they were actually time wasters doing busy work, not necessarily busy people. The mastermind group ended up being one of the best things they ever did for themselves and they were for more productive in their business for joining.

I've seen people who have reluctantly joined a mastermind group thinking they didn't really have the time…only to turn around and make sure it was the TOP priority in their business. They found it to be such a productive part of their business they made sure to clear their calendar for their mastermind sessions. They wouldn't miss if at all possible!

7. What happens if I join a group and I don't like someone in the group?

This can be a really tough one. I've had people join a group that they really like and find productive…except for that "one guy". There is one person that just drives them crazy that they really don't like.

Sometimes it's the same guy/gal for everyone. If that's the case and there is a bad apple spoiling the bunch the mastermind coach should be willing to talk to the person and either give them a change to "fix the issue", or ask them to leave the group.

There are cases that a mastermind coach is unwilling to do this. If so, sometimes the group will elect someone in the group to talk to person who is not working in the mix.

Generally, I find that the person who isn't working for some reason or another ends up leaving on their own. They usually have an attitude that doesn't mesh well with the group, and they will need to find their need met somewhere else.

Now, if it's just personal issue, that's something else. It really is a shame when you find a group that is great, but just have one person that rubs you the wrong way. Quite honestly, you only have two choices in the matter.

You can look within yourself and your business and think about what really matters. Are you gaining MORE from the group then the person is disrupting you? Is there anything you can do to tune it out? Whether its learning a mantra or doing some breathing and going to a "happy place" when the offending person is talking.

Your other choice is to find another group. It would be a shame to leave a group that is productive for you. However, if the person is getting in the way of you feeling positive, you need to go somewhere else where you can focus on staying positive and productive. The last thing you want to do is come back from a mastermind group and just think about how annoying a person was instead of the great ideas that were shared. The choice will be yours alone to make! But always speak with the coach first.

8. **I'm a very focused person – I want to make that if I join a mastermind group they are focused and I get something out of them. I can't afford to waste my time. How can I assure that my group will be productive and efficient?**

If only everything in life could be guaranteed! It's just not that easy though. Most mastermind groups do strive to be focused and productive. However, I have seen some that get sorely off track and end up being an excuse for a social occasion and simply labelled as a mastermind group. They really aren't a mastermind group at all!

When you are looking for a group, you need to interview the group just as they may interview you. Ask them what guidelines they have in place for the mastermind group. You know you're in trouble if there is a big pause followed by…"we don't really have any guidelines per se".

Also, ask what the general agenda is for the meetings. This will give you a good idea how efficient they are. Again, no agenda is a big red flag. That usually means a mastermind group that flounders for much of their time.

Ultimately, much of what you get out of a mastermind group is what you put in to it though. Going in with a positive attitude of "this is going to be a GREAT opportunity for me and my business" instead of "this had BETTER be worth it and not waste my time" makes all the difference in the world. When you are open minded and looking for positive opportunities to happen, they will come to you. You will find the nuggets instead of focusing on the negatives.

Lastly, if you do join a group that just doesn't work out for you, don't give up on mastermind groups. Just because one doesn't work doesn't mean NONE work. It's like dating…most people don't find their spouse on the first try! You may not find your perfect group on the first try either! But you're not married to a group…you can move on until you find one that is efficient and productive enough to fit your needs. Just remember to stay open minded along the way.

9. I'm an internet marketer. Why do I need a mastermind group when I can learn on the internet, go to internet marketing events or the Internet Marketers Cruise and learn from the best of the best?

This is another question I get a lot, in one form or another. The internet has truly changed business in many ways. Yes, there is a vast wealth of information available on the internet. You can do a search and come up with articles on any subject on business you could want to find. There are courses available from gurus and subject experts on every from picking a domain name to building a million dollar empire. The problem with the information on the internet is that information is the sum of total of what you get. There is no interaction. MAYBE you can ask a few questions via email or on a forum, but there is not a way to continually learn from the person who you are reading the article from in most cases (well, unless you are buying an expensive program, and even in that case, you are usually just getting DVD's of that person talking at you more.

Nothing can take the place of human interaction. Getting to know one another personally and professionally over a period of time to build trust…and then develop ideas is completely different then digesting information that is being thrust at you.

Yes, there are wonderful events that available. Not just in the internet marketing space, but in many other niches as well. There are conventions and conferences of all sorts that you can learn from the experts in your field. Often times there are networking opportunities for you to chat with them in between breaks and you may even be lucky enough to score an email exchange with someone.

But when the event is done, that is it. You've learned some great things but you don't have those people to continue to learn from and exchange ideas with and build on those ideas and see where they go.

With a mastermind group you can build trust with your group, gain insight in to new ideas that are shared, and implement those ideas in to your business. There is a place for events, conferences and networking groups in your business. Use them for what they are meant to be. A place to get some GREAT idea and network with incredible people. Just bring those great ideas back to your mastermind group, discuss them, talk about what might work, what might not, and WHY…and make a plan to implement them in to your business.

10. Once someone has achieved "success", why would they want or need a mastermind group?

This is one that I actually LIKE to hear it. To me it affords me a great opportunity to sell the benefits of a mastermind group. You see, many people assume that a mastermind group is for people who are just getting started in their business. Or for people who are "stuck". Or for people who are really struggling in a certain aspect of their business.

So the further assumption is…once someone has hit success, why would they need to stay in a mastermind group? I think we can travel all the way back to Chapter 1 for a good answer to that. Take a look at Benjamin Franklin and The Junto. Or The Inkling. What about the members of The Vagabonds? These were Presidents and heads of major companies. Successful men for sure! Just take a look at Bill Gates and Warren Buffett and work out why they meet up regularly, they are both successful? Do some homework on them and then tell me.

There are MANY successful men today who are in mastermind groups. We talked about Jay Abrahams, Rich Schefren, Dan Kennedy, Frank Kerns and more. Jack Canfield, author of Chicken Soup for the Soul is in a mastermind group. So is well known business author John Assaraf. When these people decide to get together in a mastermind group, it's not to just to help the underprivileged! They ALL believe in mastermind groups themselves! While many of them are mastermind coaches, they BELONG to mastermind groups as well.

Why? Well, let me ask you this. What is "success" to you? Is it a certain amount of money? To some people it is. To others is may be growing a business to a level of success, and then turning ANOTHER business in to a success.

Success for someone may be running a multi million pound business for 20 years – and then for the next 10 years "success" is starting a charity, or travelling the world, or figuring out how to be a better grandparent or a cook.

In our lives there really is no end to success. We just change what our next success is going to be. So the answer to the question is, when someone TRULY understands the power and the experience of the mastermind…and they have hit "success", they DO still desire to belong to a mastermind group. Most people have a hard time letting go of being a part of mastermind group when they have really found the magic that they can create in their business and their life. They simply look for a mastermind group that will meet their needs for their next phase.

> *"Never, never, never give up"*
>
> - Winston Churchill